A WORD IN MY MOUTH

The Poiema Poetry Series

Poems are windows into worlds; windows into beauty, goodness, and truth; windows into understandings that won't twist themselves into tidy dogmatic statements; windows into experiences. We can do more than merely peer into such windows; with a little effort we can fling open the casements, and leap over the sills into the heart of these worlds. We are also led into familiar places of hurt, confusion, and disappointment, but we arrive in the poet's company. Poetry is a partnership between poet and reader, seeking together to gain something of value—to get at something important.

Ephesians 2:10 says, "We are God's workmanship..." *poiema* in Greek—the thing that has been made, the masterpiece, the poem. The Poiema Poetry Series presents the work of gifted poets who take Christian faith seriously, and demonstrate in whose image we have been made through their creativity and craftsmanship.

These poets are recent participants in the ancient tradition of David, Asaph, Isaiah, and John the Revelator. The thread can be followed through the centuries—through the diverse poetic visions of Dante, Bernard of Clairvaux, Donne, Herbert, Milton, Hopkins, Eliot, R. S. Thomas, and Denise Levertov—down to the poet whose work is in your hand. With the selection of this volume you are entering this enduring tradition, and as a reader contributing to it.

—D. S. Martin
Series Editor

COLLECTIONS IN THIS SERIES INCLUDE:

Six Sundays toward a Seventh by Sydney Lea
Epitaphs for the Journey by Paul Mariani
Within This Tree of Bones by Robert Siegel
Particular Scandals by Julie L. Moore
Gold by Barbara Crooker

A Word in My Mouth

Selected Spiritual Poems

ROBERT CORDING

CASCADE *Books* • Eugene, Oregon

A WORD IN MY MOUTH
Selected Spiritual Poems

The Poiema Poetry Series

Copyright © 2013 Robert Cording. All rights reserved. Except for brief quotations in critical publications or reviews, no part of this book may be reproduced in any manner without prior written permission from the publisher. Write: Permissions, Wipf and Stock Publishers, 199 W. 8th Ave., Suite 3, Eugene, OR 97401.

Cascade Books
An Imprint of Wipf and Stock Publishers
199 W. 8th Ave., Suite 3
Eugene, OR 97401

www.wipfandstock.com

ISBN 13: 978-1-62032-965-8

Cataloging-in-Publication data:

Cording, Robert.

   A word in my mouth : selected spiritual poems / Robert Cording.

   xii + 182 p. ; 23 cm.

   The Poiema Poetry Series

   ISBN 13: 978-1-62032-965-8

   1. Poetry. 2. Christian poetry, American. I. Title. II. Series.

PS3553 O6455 W50 2013

Manufactured in the USA

Acknowledgments

The poems in this book were selected from the following books, whose publishers the author wishes to thank:

Life-list (Ohio State University Press, 1987)
What Binds Us To This World (Copper Beech Press, Brown University, 1991)
Heavy Grace (Alice James, 1996)
Against Consolation (CavanKerry Press, 2001)
Common Life (CavanKerry Press, 2006)
Walking with Ruskin (CavanKerry Press, 2011)

The author also wishes to thank the following magazines in which the poems in this book first appeared: *The American Scholar; Boston College Magazine; Boston Review; Christianity and Literature; Cimarron Review; Cortland Review; Doubletake; Georgia Review; Gettysburg Review; Green Mountains Review; Image; Indiana Review; Iron Horse Review; Kenyon Review; The Nation; New England Review; New Virginia Review; Orion; Paris Review; Post Road; Ploughshares; Poetry; Quarterly West; Sewanee Review; Southern Poetry Review; Southern Review; Spiritus; Tar River Poetry; Tiferet; TriQuarterly.*

Contents

To My Soul | 1

from *Life-List* (1987) | 3

Christmas, 1954 | 5
A Boy Adds Black Vultures To His Life-list | 6
The Horses | 8
Another Illustration | 11
Stieglitz and O'Keeffe: Appropriations | 13
Exterior View with Goldfinch | 15

from *What Binds Us To This World* (1991) | 17

All Souls' Morning | 19
Clonmacnois: A Short History | 21
After Dante | 23
Noli Me Tangere: San Marco, Florence | 25
Piero Della Francesca: The Flagellation | 26
September 3 | 28
Circles | 30
Hurricane | 33
Rock of Ages | 37
Niagara Falls | 38
Going to Sea in a Sieve | 42

from *Heavy Grace* (1996) | 45

Cardinal | 47
For Rex Brasher, Painter of Birds | 49

Washing the Body | 55
After the Funeral | 56
The Cup | 58
The Mouth of Grief | 59
Unfinished Sampler | 61
Good Friday | 63
Reading Emerson | 65
Instinct | 67
Pilgrimage | 69
Glosses | 70

from *Against Consolation* (2001) | 73

Self-Portrait | 75
Questions | 76
Nests | 77
Gift | 79
Against Consolation | 81
Gratitude | 84
Kafka and the Rabbi of Belz | 86
Moths | 88
Sam Cooke: Touch the Hem of His Garment | 90
Pause | 92

from *Common Life* (2006) | 95

A Prayer to Adam | 97
Luther and the Devil | 98
Peregrine Falcon, New York City | 100
Yard Sale | 102
Visitations | 104
Sanctuary | 106
Hummingbird Annunciation | 108
Rosary Bead, Netherlands, c. 1500 | 110
Parable of the Moth | 112
Talking Through a Storm | 113
Christmas Soccer Game, 1915 | 118
My Uncle's Parrot | 120
Lenten Stanzas | 122

Skellig Michael | 125
Advent Stanzas | 129
Sullenness | 134
Sacraments | 136
Ode to Ordinariness | 137
Pigeon Man | 139
Lord God Bird | 141
Common Life | 143
Pentecost in Little Falls, New Jersey | 144
Ears of the Heart | 147
The Weeper | 149

from *Walking with Ruskin* (2011) | 151

Dangling | 153
Thirty-Second Concert | 154
Czeslaw Milosz's Glasses | 156
Reading George Herbert | 159
Erasure | 161
Shame | 162
Sparrows | 164
Four Prayers | 166
Why I Live Here | 170
My Neighbor's Mailbox | 172
Last Things | 174
Luna Moths | 176
Gift | 178

In Between | 181

For Robert and Muriel Cording

> *What should I say about life?—that it is long*
> *and abhors transparence. Yet until brown clay*
> *has been crammed down my larynx, only gratitude*
> *will be gushing from it.*
> —Joseph Brodsky

> *Every day the glory is ready to emerge from debasement.*
> —Rabbi Nachman of Bratslav

> *I said to my soul be still and wait without hope*
> *For hope would be hope of the wrong thing; wait without love*
> *For love would be love of the wrong thing; there is yet faith*
> *But the faith and the love and the hope are all in the waiting.*
> —T.S. Eliot, *Four Quartets*

To My Soul

Despite the nay-sayers who are sure
you cannot be found and never existed
in the first place; despite thinking
once that making my soul would be easy
as I sat mumbling to myself, trying to
inhale *Jesus* and exhale *mercy* in a prayer;
despite the time I lodged in the belly
of the whale, devoured by my rage
of all that failed me in my life, by everyone
else's smallness and then, more terribly,
my own; despite my hunchbacked hopes
for everything I never had and my attempts
to build a house of many rooms only to find
my claustrophobic self in each one; despite
the lamps and the books and the ponderous
thoughts late at night and despite being
one of those apostles who so clearly
never got it right, asking all the wrong questions,
fishing in the wrong places, running away;
and despite all those moments when I
confused contentment with self-deception
and those times when all I could feel
was my own flesh lying under its stone,
pinned down by oblivion; despite all this
and despite my silly mistaken belief
that I would find you, you have waited patiently,
as if your presence—how else could so much
have been bearable?—were obliged all this time.
O my soul, the mystery is not that you exist,
but that you never abandoned me
who took so long to realize you were never

lost. How did you ever go on believing in
the minuscule chance that your prodigal son
might someday return through your open-
hearted doors to a feast already prepared.
The Lord is your portion, you whispered,
and as I ate, I wept, seized with gratitude
for a common phoebe that flew out and back,
out and back, from a newly planted tree.

from *Life-List* (1987)

Christmas, 1954

The season of peace upon us, my mother would sing
through her chores, her step lighter, and forgive us
more quickly. She would bring back the little town
under the trees, effortlessly, first the cottony snow,
then the treasured wooden houses that were her mother's,
and then the manger, so strangely natural amid the odd
assortment of Swiss chalets and half-timbered Tudor
houses which were like the houses we looked at
on long Sunday drives after church. Once a year
she laid out the streets and the tidy little shops
and the hills beyond where children sledded or
skated gaily on the pond which was once a mirror.
She must have had the impossible town in her mind
always, for there was never any hesitation as to why
something should be *here* and not *there*. The band
always played music (despite the snow) on the corner
where two streets crossed. And everyone stopped
and listened as if their work could wait forever.
Somehow it all made sense. Inside the barn,
cows and horses and oxen and sheep rested together
and the child lay perfectly happy in the straw bed.
Often I'd think of my mother's favorite stories,
miracles of water turning to wine or five thousand
fed from five loaves and fishes. More than once
in that short season, I heard Mary singing above
his bed, though the voice was always reminiscent
of my mother's, half-familiar and half-strange,
the one always turning into the other, like a dream
of a kingdom converging upon the poverty of a barn.

A Boy Adds Black Vultures To His Life-list

In the dusk of late spring,
a summer sun already taken hold,
undergrowth grown up,
birds disembodied, uninterpreted voices
behind a scrim of leaves,
I am out walking with the sunlit colors
of cardinal, goldfinch, scarlet tanager
blossoming from my bird book.
I step into a kind of clearing, some lost orchard
now a briary of vines and trees
crossed in tangle. What comes next,
comes as something I have never seen.
More body than wing, they lift
their long naked necks, their terrible heads,
then, held together
as if by design, they hunch again
over a doe, the awful exposure
of her white underside.
I see them as a Sunday school play—
the shadows behind the white sheet,
a tableau of bodies bent with unforgiven feelings.
Then I am running with a sudden force,
my arms lifted in anger. As I run,
it rises inside me again—
both frightened parents are holding my arms,
I am screaming *I hate you, I hate you both*,
and vowing never to forgive…
When they break with awkward grace
into the air, I see the extent
of their wings. As they turn wider and wider arcs,
the sun defines the sheen
of white and the darker secondaries.
For a long time I just stand there,
watching how their bodies fit the sky,

lightened now, like the sun ballooning at the horizon,
or the wind rising to redress the trees.

The Horses

> *During the nineteenth century, the steamer Royal Tar
> exploded and sank off the coast of Matinicus, Maine.
> Its cargo was a circus.*

A common enough sky, washed out with fog,
the air gray, slightly surging, though still innocent
of wind, holds no signs. There is a sun,
slight, falling, which could be a moon
in cloud, irising the gray. It is late April.
There have been the usual winter deaths
and the ground finally has been opened.
Below the cemetery, serviceable, white
boats push against the docks,
their heavy lines rising in unison
with the monotony of water.
Cod are routinely unloaded.
A woman pulls in damp wash. Along the rocks,
a small tightly grouped flock of scoters,
some sooty cormorants, and lines of eiders
in labored flight. Into sun, and down
a perfectly straight road,
a man takes his scheduled walk.
Which means it is Saturday,
and the minister sees in the sea
another image for tomorrow's service:
a rowboat checking traps, moving orderly
from one hold to the next.
A moment ago, while the minister was thinking
of a fossil, a sea animal he found
miles inland, in a bog so thicketed,
trees are marked,
a young boy carrying wood and dreaming
of migrations, of warblers

and their exotic fleshes of color,
saw the minister's frocked coat flame in the sun.

*

First, a baby crying, the sea changing
the rhythm of her breathing,
and then one yellowed light after another wakes
behind the windows. Just wind
but even the children know wind belongs to a system
of things: their school the lumber of a brig,
and this winter bales of linen, molasses, coal—
enough for every family.
So the whole island rises to that expectation.
The sea is queer. Eastward, across the inflamed
distance, the water is lurid with color.
The men guess possibilities. All night
they huddle on the ledges. The sky is more alive
than they have known, primaried with reds,
yellows, and blues. Cries of strange animals
fill the caves of their bodies.
At dawn they can see the exploded remains
of a steamer, its legend
just visible, and closer, two great white horses
climbing from the sea like nothing at all
to stand on the tide-washed rocks,
their eyes round, boldly convex,
their huge backs quivering,
their muscled flanks slick, still flared.

*

For five days bits of giraffe, hyenas, lions
have come ashore. The men have not gone
to their boats. Their wives are different.
The minister is walking toward the bog
where the florid bloom of skunk cabbage

is everywhere. There is a rich smell
of forsythia and the sea, sunlit,
Caribbean blue, is bottomless, open and swaying.
Out along the shore, near a calliope, a naked boy
watches as a girl slowly turns all of her new body
toward him. He touches the swelling flesh of her breast,
but really it's more, it's everything he ever dreamed.

Another Illustration

Though May, the air has the quality of summer,
the slow peace of a day
moving towards an evening thunderstorm.
It is evening, but the sky is still
a soft wash of pinks
coloring the brown mud tracked with random symmetries
of fox, plover, marten, and pipers.
It has already taken in
the dry yellows of last year's grasses,
the hints of green budding along the shore
where a white pine has fallen,
blacked with lightning, and now is crossing
the blue-gray water, as yet unbloomed with lilies,
towards where I am sitting in a boat
my neck reddening with mosquitoes.

This afternoon I had my first fight
with my new wife. Her cheeks flushed with anger,
then tears. I looked back
across the room before leaving,
clumsy with conflicts.

But now I am watching a snipe, and imagining
how if I were to paint it, the focus
would be its reflection, seen before the bird
in this light.
Its marshy browns, greens, and grays are a wonder
but I already know how the hawk
darkening the reflection is a match
and how nothing is quite perfect.

Which is why I wait for another illustration.
And why when the hawk's fall, like sudden rain,
is complete, I'd allow everything to settle

before making a small, reddish spot
in the lower corner of the perfectly white canvas.

From there I'd brush in
the marshy tufts of brown-green grass,
the water, still a winter-gray, though softened
by the way it complements the sky, opalescent,
tinged with warm flushes of pink
which fight my original mark to a balance,
and which are not unlike
the color of my neck when I imagine
my wife gently washing away the blood.

Stieglitz and O'Keeffe: Appropriations

I. Fall At Lake George

In the doorway, waving, he is caught
by the friendly scale of meadows and mountains
small enough for the eye to take hold of.
He notes the ministering light, how it pools
shadows into little lakes on the gradual slopes
where beautifully obedient trees
turn to reds, to yellows, to quiescent golds.

She hones the shore path with hurry,
wanting the birches, the way just now they fly
over the water, running wind
through their leaves until they seem a corona
into which she looks, the yellow-gold flares
a fever she never wants to break.

He offers a cup of coffee on her return.
In the meadow they lean back to back.
Islands tender to the lake like kindnesses,
harbors for wind-tipped waves headed home.
Mountains measure the water all around,
a fit too good to believe.

She thought this morning: how do they get there,
these moths globed inside all the lights?
She thinks of them again for a moment,
looking past the birches she has imagined
being hemmed with snow, upwards
to the urgent sounds crossing the sky as geese,
high overhead, using all their bodies in flight.

II. Photographs

In that museum room of portraits,
each part of the memorized O'Keeffe resolved
to life size, we talked in whispers
about love, his urge to record her entire:
the down on her upper lip,
the black patch of familiar hair
under her arms.

We never spoke of how his eyes
must have queried her,
choreographing the chameleon face
and the hands, the endless versions:
a wood of thin birches in passing sun,
a pair of wings going away,
or silhouetted, each finger edged with light,
floating so purely they seem unable to be held.

Exterior View with Goldfinch

(after seeing Fairfield Porter's work)

For days now, in the yellow light,
goldfinches have leaned into the forgotten
sunflowers, their yellow bills opening
black seeds, their yellow and black
bodies more than their usual colors
in the flattening August sun.
After a while I thought that painting
this, you would have wanted everything
to count equally: the light, the bills,
the seeds both before and after opening.

In *Still Life With White Boats*,
the foreground and background are all
wrong, the far-away boats almost the same
size as the closer pitcher and its bay
of blue. There's nothing between
the still life inside and those boats
except the even light and the strong focus
of early fall, a day in late afternoon
when the usual birches, the burnt-orange
meadow, the water all look significantly

closer. It's said that breakthroughs
are mostly accidental, the obvious seen again
in a new light: Now some scientists see
the plumage of birds as such a rich surface
that its worth must lie simply in the visible
appearance. These goldfinches are lovely.
I wrote about them to a friend, beginning
"Nothing much has happened here . . . ."
Nothing has, but I suspect you'd understand
how such days go on to make a life.

from *What Binds Us To This World* (1991)

All Souls' Morning

County Kerry, Ireland

Jittery light, scraps of wind, the monotone of rain.
Is it the thrushes moving across the poor cloth
of grass that brings my grandmother to the margin
of memory? I'd come from classes twice a month

to eat with her. All those women, moving in unison,
fitting and stitching. Clattering machines. "Piece-work,"
my grandmother called it. She's back at work again,
tethered this time to her husband's death. In the dark

she rises to cook breakfast for two. Later she dusts
his pictures, habits of grief shaping her round of days.
She tends the dead the way these cows in their pendulous
plodding way cross from unlit barn to field, that haze

of expectation always in their wet eyes. They stand
and feed, nuzzle the short, depleted grass into milk.
Mornings I bring my small faith to the close at hand;
just now the blued iridescent wing of a common rook

offers itself to my eye. Sparks of flinty sun.
Gone in rain's let-downs. Glimmerings and blurs.
On time, the co-op tractor stops in the stubborn rain,
here to collect the morning's milk. A widow, two doors

down, will invite the driver in for tea. "They'll marry,"
my neighbor's said, his eyes kindling with the thought
of their rising again from hurts. And him, he's "lucky
to have a good job"; he waves hello now through the mist

and I see again how his face, reddish-yellow, is raw

from the chemicals he handles. After his lungs gave
way to asbestos-crazed cells bred thirty years before
in the rat-gray dark of a second job he had to have,

my grandfather said, "Hell, the pay was good and when
I came up from the dark, the cars and dirty roads
were never brighter, never as clear." Wind and rain,
smoke and mist, spots of sun interceding like words

that rise up at oddest moments to make the world
always there suddenly apparent. Quick as breath,
the hours go by, a rook sweeps sideways on wind,
threads a needle's hold of light as if on faith.

The world keeps moving to its tasks, random with pain,
rich with surprise. The tractor's gone off with milk,
the cows turn to shoots of grass raised by the rain,
I write: *In backlit mist, the thrushes' feathers are silk.*

Clonmacnois: A Short History

It's deserted except for the light
gliding over exhausted stone, the rain
that wakes a steam of ghosts above

the grass. Rooks grip the wind's edge,
wishbones of lightning break against
the black wings of trees, and the sky

floods with sun and storm. There are
two towers, eight ruined churches,
three crosses, a vast field of graves

like volumes of history too numerous
for anyone to make sense of.
Centuries ago this city was a vision,

Saint Ciaran opening his eyes on
a huge flowering tree, its fruitful
branches a place for birds to come and eat.

A monastery grew up, drew boatloads
of students who wanted to climb
ladders of wisdom, to learn the love

of saints. There were raids, fires,
plunderings—a thousand years of violence,
a thousand years of prayers for love

to match it. Saint Ciaran appeared
for centuries, looming up at marauders,
carrying his crozier as if to heal them:

a story which took years to imagine,
which was needed to balance the raids

that kept coming. This city was lost

and saved and lost again, preserved now
in ruin. Only the stories continue:
some see horrible scenes of slaughter

in the night sky above Clonmacnois;
others see boats, yearning upwards,
sails filled with star-pearled air.

After Dante

It was in Verona. I had just been
to Dante's statue
and, standing there, alone with him
in the center of the square,

I had almost believed in the light again
wheeling in a heaven
that smiled. I had almost believed
in the stars again and the love
that moved them,
that helped Dante understand the earth

he looked back upon,
remembering the injustice and the suffering
that had never made sense.

I was on the way to Saint Zeno
to feel the faith
carved in its doors, when I saw him.
He seemed as if he couldn't move, not ever.
He said nothing, just
kept to what he was doing,
his eyes enormous with his need,
the syringe he held
against his arm until he collapsed,
like a shadow after the light moves away.

I think now he needed me
the way those locked in hell needed Dante
to tell their story.
So I have, though I have no circle
to place him in, no reason even
for his being there.

Or for my leaving him lying there,
looking up at the empty table of rooftops,
what little light there was
seeping down on the twisting streets,
the featureless doorways.

Noli Me Tangere: San Marco, Florence

*The frescoes are designed to keep the scene
constantly before the monk's eyes.*
 —John Pope-Hennessey

Outside this cell the sparrows repeat
their seasonal songs.
Here a fresco to teach the soul
the same lesson over and over.

I come often. I think
of the monk who, each morning, faced
the grief of reaching out for what is always
just out of reach.

Just the other side
of Mary's outstretched hands,
Christ's trailing hand serenely denies.
His lightened body leaves no footprints

in the grass. For too many years
I have seen your hands laid at your sides,
your face which left me nothing
I could say.

In this cell, I see the monk's breath
following him as he walks.
I see how Mary keeps
entering the solitudes of grief,

her hands filling with memory
as one by one by one
those last perfect words drift beyond
her understanding.

Piero Della Francesca: The Flagellation

It might be a dream, it is so calm, so silent,
this whipping that is always
taking place under an unbroken spell of blue sky.

I look on from a distance. Like the distance between
wanting to help and helping.

I have come to think of the three men—fellow citizens?—
as a scholar, a senator, and a merchant,
if only to give substance to their oblique reverie.

Behind them, behind the pink and white buildings,
beyond the cool tiles and the columns of the piazza's
too-brilliant light (one perspective giving way to another),

two henchmen have raised whips above the human flesh—
an atrocity that seems the rumor of an atrocity
too far off to believe.

In the silence of that distance
the scholar considers the consolations of history,
each event part of a cycle that cannot be helped.

The senator tells himself he has seen it all before,
the suffering of one always lost in the suffering
too general for solution.

And the merchant reminds himself
of the accommodations that must be made
to the business of day-to-day.

We can't go as near the pain as we should.
We can't go away from it, either. In this dream
a rooster might be calling *What will you do?*

One cloud without motion in the enamel sky,
the air still as glass, the morning hour hovering.

September 3

In her parlor drinking tea, Virginia Woolf
sees how first light enters the room
like a ghost still in need of knowledge,
her wall of books lit title by title.
Now it makes a door of light
on the wall and she imagines walking through,
unscathed, and emerging in the garden
to watch a new sun steam over the horizon

of wet roofs, redden the highest apples
in the orchard, then come to rest
in the wet grass, in the cold earth's cache
of complex scents that goes on defying
her best efforts to name. The day promises
blue sky, crisp white clouds, rafts
of birds shooting the invisible currents.

In her journal, she writes: "I suppose
the bombs are falling on rooms just like this
in Warsaw. A fine sunny morning here,
apples shining."

Just those two sentences
for September 3. Perhaps she finished
her tea, went outside. Weeds, new blooms
of asters and chrysanthemums.
What else could she have done? Perhaps
a third sentence for the opposing pair
formed, revolved in her mind, and dissolved.

I imagine she sat at dusk in the orchard,
the first apples already dropped, flaming
in the grass. I imagine the earth's slow turning
was like an ache inside her,

one day undone by another, and yet each day
arriving as if it would be the day
she'd understand what happens, for what reasons.

Circles

A tractor this morning
broke my spell of words—
another version of a place
alive with family and history,
another version of a world
small enough to know.

For a moment I saw you, Earl,
green work pants and shirt,
your face streaked with dust,
and I waited for the engine
to whinny down, for your knock
at the door and the usual

request for a glass
of cold water. You're dead
two years already. It was
spring when I saw you last,
yet another day of rain.
You said your seed was rotting

in the ground. A few weeks
later I heard of your suicide.
There were signs—
your clenched face, your
hobbled words—after your father's
and then your brother's deaths,

but they didn't fit my model
of you: old world Yankee
cut from the cloth of self-
reliance, up to the absurd
trials the days deal out.
Soon I thought we'd talk again

of farms and farmers, of land
in the same family for generations.
The truth was your farm
was no more than a few poor acres
and the land you leased edged
by rows of identical houses.

Once you brought me to see
your father's house—"an old one
like your own." We made our way
through a house where nothing
was left of history except
those things we never use

but can't give up. Your father
sat by a gas heater and, despite
your on-stage cues, could not
bring about the past we wanted
to remember. I think now
that your last months were

mostly filled with shame.
After your suicide, people
who knew you said your brother
ran whatever farm there was,
that for thirty years
you'd been mostly a handyman,

a good man but a dreamer,
unable to run a farm
in this day and age. And so
you are dead. Dante found
suicides in a trackless,
knotted wood, knowing that

once hope is lost, there is
no life. From the darkness,
from the leafless trees,

came the wailings of those
enclosed. Listening, Dante
was speechless and afraid:

how close all of us come
to these woods, how quickly
our lives can collapse. Who can
walk through hell without seeing
sins that are his own, without
stumbling in fear and sympathy?

What got Dante through hell
was mostly faith, I think
that he could learn and change.
At first I wanted these lines
to circle back at last
to spring (here, the farmers

turn their hardened fields).
But the spring you hanged yourself
the muddy fields spoke only
of the likelihood of failure,
the willows' yellow-greens
burst forth like shame.

There's no telling how spring
will return or when your hopes
will be seen too fully
for the lies they mostly are.
It's spring. Fortunate enough
to have another chance,

I'm trying to live in the world
and not my version of the word.
I lay down these small lines
like furrows in the field.
Call it hope. Or the chance
of hope. For both our sakes.

Hurricane

Forecast, the hurricane arrives
right on schedule:

first the amplified wind,
the over-dramatic soliloquies

of oaks and maples,
and then the steeped sky,

pinched silvery green air
crackling with rain.

Bat-size leaves fly at windows
crossed and recrossed

with tape. The power goes off
but returns. On the TV

pictures of what's happening
this very minute:

some "crazy" surfers
we're not supposed to emulate

are trying to put on
the storm's power.

Sixty miles inland, I put on
my rain gear and go outside,

crazy for extremities.
Seventy times its usual self

but still not the animal
thing I've imagined,

all claw and crushing power,
the wind, rain-slashed but balmy,

breaks around me
in the early false dark.

Suddenly I see myself
as I must look

to my bewildered neighbors—
a suburban Ulysses

who hopes to appropriate
the siren calls

of pines planted in rows
to break the noise of trucks

and passing cars.
Full of the shame of one

who must learn the same lessons
over and over,

those first months
in the South of Ireland come back

at me: my perverse envy
of lives far enough away

to be dramatic,
to take form as allegory,

violence a story told
in a bar, distant, mythologized.

Because I wanted more
than the everyday

ordinariness of being American,
because I wanted to write bolder

lines in touch with
the stray chatter of gunfire

on any given day, I didn't see
the cycle of irredeemable deaths,

one man traded for another . . .
This far north and inland,

the hurricane revved up
like a teenager starting

his father's car in the driveway,
then resigned itself

to pick-up sticks of asters
and chrysanthemums,

dead branches
creasing still-green lawns

and a few upended
shallow-rooted pines.

Now: gusts of freighted air,
sudden lulls,

the hurricane backing off
like a neighborhood dog.

Embryonic light brightens
a ceiling of gray sky.

First birds move
to their appointed tasks:

a phoebe flies out
and back, out and back.

A towhee returns
to its small persistence

in the fallen leaves.
And now a chainsaw starts up,

a neighbor hauls a wheelbarrow
full of blow-down.

"Lucky," he shouts,
"we're lucky," and turns

back to his work.
Gradually we return

to a world we never left
which seems, on our return,

to take on a meaning
that involves our being here,

if only to give thanks,
if only to note the daily

geese dropping earthward
in ones and twos,

settling on a field
of leveled corn rows

that could be but are not
a field of innocent dead.

Rock of Ages

My grandmother, just back from the hospital,
her heart lost and returned for a fourth time,
sings "Rock of Ages," her voice quavering,
graceless, yet determined still to bring
her great-grandson, cranky and tired, to his rest.
His unaged face lies against her
as mine must have when I listened to
the same words floating in air, calling on Christ
to help us in our helplessness. In her voice
I hear her first husband—drunk, raging—
whom she loved and prayed would die.
I hear my grandfather, her second husband,
who provided until he took cancer home
from his job, his lungs a wound that wouldn't heal.
I hear the ghost who wants to lie down
with her now each time she sleeps. I hear
her heart that should have ended but has not,
that sings as if time can only bring pain
and a way to take it away. Outside
the afternoon is locked in gray,
little difference between what lies ahead
and what's already past. Mourning doves
make their sounds of love or sadness.
Of both or neither. I think of the times
when, trembling, I have sung this hymn
in which Christ's wound is a place to hide,
where rabbits and moles, hedgehogs
and bears sleep peacefully in a view of earth
we otherwise never get to see.

Niagara Falls

For miles the high power relay stations
pointed to the Falls. No honeymooners,
we were driving west to show your family

our first child, bound and wailing
in his car seat. The Falls were just a place
to spend the night, a place almost too apt

for easy cynicism: hadn't I heard
a historian mourn the loss of the Falls
as symbol—the Sublime gone the American way

of tourists and shoppers wandering
in an Eden of happy consumption . . . Dusk
before we got around to seeing the Falls.

Inside the park, lovers and families
strolled with the usual fare of Cokes,
french fries, hot dogs, or took pictures

of themselves looming in front
of the diminished Falls. I tried to imagine
the first terrifying looks at the Sublime—

the vastness and power, the obscuring mist,
the incessant roar, the distance
the mind had to cross to compass its dimensions—

but the river, looked at from the guardrails,
only seemed to slow, the rapids sliding by
in long, polished runs, the precipice

of plunging water like the enormous brow
of a friendly giant who lived in the mist,
who smiled when the clouds opened their gates

and the sky let down only a cordial light.
We had to admit there was a dizzy pleasure
in the plunging water, the rising mist,

the bunches of onlookers adding their summery
colors to the evening. We held our child up
to see the view. Close by another couple

embraced, kissed urgently. I thought of
a night when I lay in bed listening to you
in another room, your coos melodying

our son's satisfaction at your breast.
I thought of how I waited for you to return,
to be, I'll admit my childish jealousies,

my wife again, though I knew that evening
we were parents, mother and father,
connected in ways we hadn't imagined,

that demanded a revision of ourselves
to each other . . . Five years have passed.
We've added two children, revisited the Falls

only in paintings. His canvas eight-feet wide,
Church's vantage point was the vertigo
of power, the horizon where the sky met

the manifest destiny of water.
An image for a nation that saw itself
in God's eyes, that, blessed, completed

the impossible Erie Canal, shouldered aside
the Niagara's river behind a dam;
from a bridge's expanse, looked down

on the river. Now what's left
is the park beside the Falls, wilderness
become landscape. There's a painting

by Kensett in which the fall of water
is hardly noticed and yet it's there,
seen from a distance, like the perspective

of age that takes for granted loss
and the revision of our dreams, the grand
flights of the mind come to rest

in the obdurate particulars of day-to-day.
For Kensett, the sun leans its light
on the simple convictions of falling

water and the shorelines of leafy oaks
and willows that grow around the rapids
that hold the Falls so tenderly,

as if they'd learned how to cherish
what binds us to this world.
It's a landscape more intimate

for his choosing. Our lives have taken on
such intimacy. And it would be good
to end here with Kensett's Falls speaking

in words of tenderness and encouragement.
But the greatest riches go on inspiring
the greatest plunder. That great landscape

has been shackled in high tension wires
and lit with motel signs that outbid
each other with offers of TV, cable, ad

XXX movies. It's a country that still wants
to believe, like a schoolyard bully,
in its own exaggerations of dominance.

A country that keeps me reaching back to
the past so I can bring forward that moment
when, in the wet, neoned parking lot

of our motel, I heard the Falls, if only
on faith, under the hiss of rain-slick tires
and remembered how I'd flushed with warmth

when earlier you'd said "I love you"—no matter
the countless honeymooners who had whispered
the same words, no matter what had been lost

in the view we chose for ourselves and our son—
as we stood, among the crowds, taking in
the Falls from the less spectacular American side.

Going to Sea in a Sieve

> *One of my favorite books is a little book by*
> *an English scientist for children on soap bubbles.*
> *—Elizabeth Bishop*

    The soap bubble forms
like a perfect glass model of earth—
it's only soapy water and the breath
      and strength of

    a boy's attention
as he leans out his bedroom window
somewhere in France in an age valuing
      the large myths

    of monumental paintings.
"*Les bouteilles de savon,*" Chardin called
it. The critics knew he painted only
      the close at hand

    world he knew,
beautifully enough and with rapt
devotion to detail, but a world,
      nevertheless,

    too common.
In his book, *Soap bubbles*, C.V. Boys
wonders how water holds the world's
      shape. The scientist

    calls the child
in us back to our first *why's*. Back
to the observable mysteries of facts.
      The first lesson

  makes us see
the surface of water, its skin. Boys
sets a sieve (with eleven thousand holes)
  on the water's

  glassy sea. It
floats! The words of a nursery rhyme
become actual things: a pipe for a mast,
  a sail made

  of a pea-green veil
a ribbon for rigging. Two wooden figures
stand in for us and go to sea in a sieve.
  (See Figure 6.)

  A storm might sink
them, of course. They're no more safe
than we are, walking around on land
  with all the old

  sicknesses and
accidents plus the new ones we've added—
chemicals, cancers, terrorists, the bomb.
  The scientist would

  not say otherwise.
Yet his warm devotion to the common
miracle of water keeps us afloat.
  And it's the boy

  we admire as he shapes
his own breath into the precarious
configuration called a soap bubble.
  All his life goes

  into that moment
of attention. How steady his look
and his crossed hands that hold the rod
  from which the

  beautiful,
shimmering surface of the bubble depends!

from *Heavy Grace* (1996)

Cardinal

For a week of mornings, the cardinal came
to the window's glassy face and stalled there,
its tail and wings sculling, its beak and chest
stuttering against the dead end of glass.
It flew to its image as if it were real,
the window giving back the self the bird
couldn't reach or get away from. Summer,
mid-July, one day bound to another by a sun
like a silver mesmerizing coin, appearing,
disappearing, hours ticking in a spell of heat.

My Aunt, her cancer jabbing like a fist
in her spine, woke each morning to a face
gaping back, "Can that be me?" Strapped in
a wheelchair, doubled over, drugged with pain,
she asked, "What did I do to deserve this?"
That last month of her life her voice
and the psalmists I studied filled my head,
all of them vexed, calling out, "O Lord,
why art thou so far from helping me?"

Inside myself, I looked out at her pain,
at the cardinal caught in its pool of glass.
Once, the cardinal witlessly knocking
at the window, I chased its image with my own.
Startled, it flew off, a tongue of flame.
That July I read the Psalms, then Bonhoeffer
who found the heart cannot be comforted,
such comfort requiring we no longer see ourselves.

My Aunt died in pain. Eighty-three years,
a life long enough for her mourners who came
and went easily. The minister ignored
the life lost to speak of the life to come.

I thought of a heaven of seraphs, psalmists
who burst perpetually into flame as they sing—
the imagining of men who have sensed
what it might be to step clear through
the mirror of themselves and begin, here, now.

For Rex Brasher, Painter of Birds

> *They are gallant children, living the few swift hours*
> *of life with courage rarely attained by mortals.*
>   —Rex Brasher

I.

This shortened day of wind-flickered yellow-oranges
and golds, of the sumac's heart-colored incandescent glow,

is like a lifetime compressed into a kiss, given
and received by the dying.

A quick-setting sun in the west, a waxing moon in the east.
Already the indelible outline of the invisible

fullness to come circled on the sky's darkening shimmer.
Instant by instant, everything intensifies—

phoebes sieve the air for insects on the verge
of disappearing and a squirrel, all bristling energy,
    fast-forwards

across the grass's thinning hair. Now the last eye-urging
petals of bleeding heart and the chrysanthemums'

muted rusts and yellows sharpening their color
in the deepening light. Now, the sun's softest angle opens

the spruce, edging each blue-green needle, and a flock
of sparrows release from the branches' dusky cave

into the sunlight. My mind reels like a psalmist's
stricken with wonder, beauty and terror, the world

and the otherworldly, gesturing toward a language
larger than himself. Always that task.

To conceive a figure for these bright clouds of waxwings
    dissolving
into light. As Brasher tried to do,

who wanted to paint, from life, the quiver of the kestrel,
the muscled blue arrow of the kingfisher

pulled straight to its target beneath the distorting
water. There was no end to it: 12 volumes, 90,000

hand-colored prints, 3,000 individual birds.
874 more paintings than Audubon.

And twice, each bird translated at last to paper and color,
he knew what he'd painted was less than he'd known.

One thousand watercolors destroyed.
The necessary repetitions of beginning and beginning.

II.

All last summer my grandmother died. At the edge
of her bed, I read her Psalms of praise for a world

ramified without end, which could just as well be nothing.
She descended into sadness and fear. I held her chill

hands, stroked their onion paper skin. I tried to bring
the world alive in words. Outside the swallows went

on thinking with their wings. They flashed at her window
like shadows. She wouldn't look out. I kept wanting

what she didn't have and I couldn't give: words
that could turn her suffering to praise. I kept pointing

away from ourselves, toward the wind's sudden
and unexpected rise into high spirits or a cardinal,

crowned and fiery, too wild and strange for the world
of cut-leafed birch. In the nursing home's long hall,

the old, lined up in wheelchairs, could have been souls
in purgatory. Their mottled arms and hands reached out

whenever a child skipped by. They'd run their hands
over my son's head, lightly, as if he were a bird

they held once, long ago. They'd speak to him in dove-like
    coos.
Each day my grandmother worried herself into the dark.

All that time I waited for a moment
when, without need, she would look neither forward nor
    back,

but grow alert to the minutest shifts of light outside
her window. At the end, I held her, I listened

to her last words—*I am*, she whispered—an answer
to my question: *Are you afraid?*

III.

He was seen standing for hours in icy water or bent
to the lettering of bird tracks in the mud, his neck bloodied

by mosquitoes. He'd walk miles or sit in one place waiting,
trying to learn the difference between possibility

and expectation, the birds always in his mind,
brush strokes and colors struggling to be visible.

Of course most days his paintings were an indictment
of his dexterity: the bullying mind omitting and deleting

or annexing whatever it needs. Not painting was worse:
an exclusion, a sadness that made the world disappear.

As if he were here to see the goldfinches' yellow and black
flight of falls and risings into paint's affirmation.

Or as if his seeing were made possible only by the
    goldfinches'
elusive riches. Of course each painting was, in time,

a disappointment. Yet whatever heaven he came to know,
he knew while painting, his heart and his hands given

to the task, say, of the twenty different tans and umbers
of the wood's understory detailed in a grouse's feathers.

Such work took all his life: ninety-one years
that began in the aftermath of the Civil War only to turn

again and again to ditches of agony where the dialogue
of God and man came to an end. He turned to birds,

their 200 million-year-old history. He saw the reptile
in their feet and eyes. And how the reptile climbed

and perched; and jumped from branch to branch.
Then glidings. Then flights. All those years to trust

the emptiness and grandeur of air. Birds:
their abundance and variation like the world's,

a world which shouldn't be but is and for no reason.

IV.

My grandmother's death just days off, the two of us wearied,
one afternoon we gave up hope for anything more

than the hours we had. We offered each other
our arms and a kiss. There was nothing else

to do. I can hardly speak of that moment. There was
the taste of her suffering and pain, and the hush of death.

There was the touch of her lips, cold, waxy, wet with spittle
and sweat. There was the darkness that rose up

to this edge of her body and also a sweetness,
as though her soul had come to rest on the crest of her

breathing. And there was the terrifying peace
of the dark wordlessness I found there and keep to this day,

the next-to-last of October, half dark, half glitter
of dissolving sun high in the green-becoming-gold tamaracks.

My children kick a ball across the lawn plumed
with fallen leaves, the taste of imminent frost in their

open mouths as it is in mine, the coming winter
a bodily knowledge. Under the trees, the pooling body of
    evening

slides beneath the afternoon like some otherworldly lover.
And the sky's last violet-reds could be the colors

of dawn on the earth's other side. Everything—
the tamaracks and maples, the spruces and their
    smoke-winged

sparrows, the painterly sky darkening toward infinity—
offers itself as a source of awe. Just now,

the more I listen, the more the geese, high overhead,
    anonymous,
speak their heart-breaking language. I do not understand,

but believe it has something to do with time, each passing
moment brief as a life, and yet time enough for a life
   to change.

Washing the Body

At the end of your life, you are all weight,
nothing in your body to help lift it at all.
There is only the empty diagram your lines
of bones and skin make, worn for eighty-one years,
but never again. Hard to believe this body
charged so through the world—this still,
it seems never to have moved at all, never
to have risen this very morning. A long day
of pulling yourself upright, letting yourself
lie down. Then it was done. No matter how
slowly death comes, it arrives all at once.
Now I run a damp cloth across your forehead,
feel a crease left by a last frown. I remove
your valuables as the nursing home instructed:
a watch that hasn't stopped, a wedding ring
inscribed with promises. I don't know what to do
with your hands. Should I fold them over you,
or lay them, open, at your sides? Lifting one
to my face, I have to hold it in place, cupped
to my ear like a shell. In your eyes,
the radius of light I knew you by glints
like a mirror in an emptied room. There is
nothing to see, yet I may never again see
it so clearly. Nothing to wish for, nothing
to will, now there is only this washing to do.

After the Funeral

    As if some force we did not recognize,
        or did not wish to,
propelled us, we moved through the afternoon,
    driving past the fronts of houses
        and their fenced dry plots

    of grass where sprinklers stammered
        under a fierce sun.
We stood at the grave, we stood in groups
    passing words between us, everything
        we did not say

    staring back in each other's faces.
        We stood there,
waiting for the moment to leave and then
    we turned back to our cars, the sun
        still pressing down

    like a stone, the light washing out
        all color, the glare
so strong we had to shield our eyes,
    or close them. Afterwards we ate
        and drank and grew sleepy.

    We slept as if great difficulties
        had been faced
and overcome, as if there was nothing
    left to do, nothing to pay
        attention to, not even

the pain we thought we had buried,
    that lived on
inside us and should have made us more
    alive than we'd ever been, focused
        the intractable present.

We slept the indolent sleep
    of grief and whiskey,
our bodies' heavy slumber like the sleep
    of those guards in Piero's fresco,
        each of them abetting

the other, all of them unable to
    move or wake
as Christ steps from his stone tomb.
    He has crossed all of night to reach
        this moment,

his face wild and fierce with his struggle,
    the inrush of light
so sudden, of such intensity, surely
    the guards must feel its pressure
        against their eyelids.

And still they lie there, so near
    and yet turned from
that face they were to watch for as the sun
    ferries its passing shadows. He must
        have known when

they'd retreat into an easier world
    and how, once
he'd slipped from their sight, they'd see
    him, time and time again, their whole
        sleepless lives.

The Cup

What longing you had to be nothing
more than the light moving
across the grass like the stateliest ship.
To move into a light you could not glimpse.
How many times in the dark
too dark to see in, death came to you,
a weightless lover, and unraveled its beautiful oasis
out of nothing for you.
And each time you must have thought, "It is right
that I go away and not return."

And yet, after the days
had lost any gleam of welcome,
after sleep had become a battle
to wake to another pain, it took only our voices
to call you back. There we sat, at your bedside,
saying your name.

As though a human voice could dispel the dream
you wanted to become the world,
you stayed. Or as though you had learned
from all those years
of sitting at dusk with neighbors,
one or two to a stoop, the close houses
like sunstruck metal giving back the day's heat,
that there is no place else to go.
Or perhaps the cup of unhappiness you drank
was not emptied
until we could say, "You must go now,
your suffering is too much for us to bear."

The Mouth of Grief

I remember how we stood there,
in that poorly lit church in Arezzo, straining
with binoculars to see *The Legend,* half worn away.

All afternoon we studied how Francesca added one scene
to the one before until it told the story

of the True Cross,
each fresco a signpost pointing the way
of a past made and corrected and made again,

without end, as though we were always bound
to discover our innocence was already marked.

We kept coming back to an old Adam
staggering under the weight of his being.

Even after he has been laid down,
his children cannot understand their father's implacable gaze.

Unimaginable. Unimaginable, that first death
until Seth, gone for oil of mercy, returns with a branch
from the Tree of Knowledge;

until that one child finds her mouth opened
against the silence of a face turned away.

From her mouth,
those first wild involuntary words must enter
the stricken landscape

no one has ever finished restoring,
their deep syntax of grief

something we must have understood even before
we could speak it.

Unfinished Sampler

In dark *Y*'s two trees divide
into two branches leafed in green
thread. Saffron for meadows
of grass, kingfisher blue
for the stream ambling through
in little stitched *x*'s.

Two black birds, curved like
a child's eyebrows, create a sky.
In tight-worked vermilion letters—
For my beloved daughter Rachel—
then the dates of her short life,
stitched by a single gathering thread

to bring together the beginning
and the end—and yet the sampler's left
incomplete. There's a fence
outlined with enough rambling roses
to scent each summer day,
though a little more than half

are left unblossomed. No way
to know why the mother forfeited
the comfort such handiwork affords.
Why her hand, poised to finish
another rose, was never lowered.
There's no sign of hurry to fill in

the silence between stitches,
no sign of a moment's irreversible
despair that there was nothing more
to hope for except the design
her hands could accomplish.
It's as if she had arrived

at a place she knew she must remain.
As if her symmetry-bound summer world
had become, in time, a reminder
of that other world Eve had to leave,
her grief never finished, an emptiness
she had to start over in each day.

Good Friday

> *Yet dare I almost be glad I do not see*
> *That spectacle of too much weight for me.*
> —John Donne, Good Friday, 1613. Riding Westward

Drab as the day itself, two phoebes,
one turning its breast against stick-ends
and sharp dry grass, the other dragging
clumps of dog hair, sheep wool, moss
from under the spruces. *A nest,*

Michelet said, *is a bird's suffering.*
All morning they've worked under
the muffled chill March sun,
their empty bowl, as likely to fall
as not in the winds to come,

taking shape on the narrow ledge
above a window. A longing
that emptiness be filled. I think
such blind urgency must have turned
John Donne that Friday he rode westward,

some longing for what he could feel
only as a loss so deep it stunned him
with its absence into words.
And now I find myself turned toward
this day I've so long forgotten,

as if my own longing were being used
to call me. Donne was almost glad
he did not see. He knew why
he wanted to look away, why he could not
look any further than the grieving

Mary bound by love to love most fully
in those unbearable hours. I cannot
say what it would mean to watch God die.
All morning I've felt again the pain
and fear in each breath used up

those last minutes of your life.
I remember the weight of your head
and the nest I tried to make of my arms.
And I remember how, with no peace
in your eyes, no words in your open mouth,

no signs nor wonder, death shuddered
its knowledge into you. Just this
once I kept death in my sight, stayed
to close its fixed and unblinking eyes.
I cannot say if you knew who I was

or even if the love I felt for you
in those last hours made any difference.
How strange still, those hours I sat
with you. Each time you cried out,
it left a mark in me. Yet the more

I entered the rawness of your pain
the more some strength of love took hold
of me. Such violence and peace
in those hours. In the end, Donne cried out
for a God strong enough to make him see.

It was the cry of his heart's longing
to turn to love, no matter the cost.
I have heard that cry this morning
as if it came from inside my own body,
as if, again, it needed a voice to speak it.

Reading Emerson

Waking in the night, I rise and pad old boards
that sound my passage in the dark. A mirror

stops me cold—floats back a shadow-body,
a glinting stooped likeness, here and not here,

crosshatched by tree branch and moonlight.
We *haunt our lives*—Emerson comes back

from my afternoon's reading. Outside,
five dwarf apple trees shadow the grass.

Two deer have come to eat the windfalls.
They draw the shadows around themselves,

become the trees: quick-muscled limbs
all slow motion, each leaf noise held in

articulated ears. Now three more inscribe
themselves on the pearled edge of grass.

Why do I want to clap my hands, whistle, hoot,
anything to make them move? Their patience tires.

Back in bed, the light's unassignable moment
by moment evolution begins, the sky graying.

Every look should thrill—Emerson again,
that *should* a stone his sentence trips over,

a hard reminder of how the world keeps slipping
from attention. Soon the moon will pass

into the opening mouths of birds whose songs
will break this darkness. Soon the deer

will vanish as if they were never here,
as if they are a dream I will wake from

when I rise again, nothing here but shadows
thrown by the apple trees on which the sun falls.

Instinct

Big, baggy clouds and a small breeze,
        custodial, going over and over
              the fields with a whisk broom's
    resolute, quick strokes. With an ant's devotion
        it carried off bits and pieces
of old newspaper, last year's leaves, husks and
        shells of winter's detritus.

Everywhere the natal tinge of April:
        in the blushing red-tipped maples,
            in the willows' delicate yellow,
    in the fields' patchy first greens (where snow
        lay a week ago). Nothing linear
in this plot—repetitive, demanding, April's
        childish light surges in

and again I find myself
        walking toward the river.
            Strange to be drawn so,
year after year, by such mindless resurrections,
        meaningless some would say
when the earth itself is no longer certain
        of abiding. Helpless,

it seems, to change my migratory route,
        I walk toward the river's
            line of oaks, their leaves
    still clenched, though the branches shine
        and shiver as if in premonition.
Back home, the phoebes, oddly human, inhabit
        the small, livable space

above the downspout (I've found
        what may be my own hair

lining their woven nests).
Here the redwings fuss for attention,
raising tricolor flags.
Near the river, I flush a killdeer and watch
its deliberate solicitude.

It flutters, it drags one wing,
then another. It refuses to fly
off, staking its claim
to an invisible ring of near-mathematical
precision around the hidden
nest. Devotion? Mere instinct? Young,
full of myself

and undergraduate knowledge,
I used to say depth of feeling
depends on consciousness.
But years and one failed marriage past,
I held my just-born son,
bloody still, to my lips—and stepped beyond
the threshold of thought,

the doors of my heart unhinged.
I would have laid down my life
for this seconds-old child
I didn't know. I cannot ignore these times
when my body takes the lead,
and I arrive at these greenish loops of water
where a heron lifts and

extends one foot so hypnotically time
seems without meaning and then,
so quickly only my senses follow,
strikes through its reflection and raises,
from the river's understory,
a fish, quivering now like something essential
the mind comes back to.

Pilgrimage

    They are born for this: to leave
        in the pre-dawn cold. Every year
without knowing, they come to the day
    when they must set out. Now
        again, the machine of the seasons
turns its gears and geese form

    my attention. Like us, they
        repeat themselves, always
something they are trying to reach,
    something they are trying to get
        away from. Years ago,
I saw how the summer weekends

    beckoned with their cool nights
        in the mountains, with the wind
blowing in at the shore. Each weekend
    the procession of cars. The transient
        red tinge of brake lights,
exhaust, watery heat. The sound

    of tires like the sound of waves
        turned once toward the moon,
once toward the earth. Always the promising
    future reassembling itself
        as the past, as the time
it took for the shuttling pilgrimage.

    Always the nights when I'd hear
        only the tidal migration of passing
cars, a dream I could not wake from,
    nor understand, and yet I knew,
        even as a child, it had to do
with the ache of something missing.

Glosses

After the 9TH century Irish monastic poems

First light breaking the silence between
the last night sounds and the first

mourning dove's *who, who, who.*

Mist in the trees, sun in the mist
saying itself like a word coming clear.

At once, dispersal: veery and thrush,
white-throat and tanager.

A pair of yellow warblers flaring
from branch to branch, too quick
for my eyes to hold, blinking in the sun.

* * *

In intervals between passing clouds—
patches of sunlight, fresh blue
of roadside delphiniums.

Eight syllables
of a white-throated sparrow come clear

across the field to where I sit, wordless,
paper and pencil in my lap. Eight syllables,

its syntax
a sentence I know, but have not found
words for.

* * *

Speed of a hummingbird's line
in air from wood edge to daylily
and back. Canyons between pines
where light hasn't reached yet;
and a thrush, ventriloquial,
throwing its voice from far back
or near: that story
of a monk who stopped to listen
to a bird's call in the forest.
Returning to the monastery gate,
he found no one who remembered him
he had been gone so long.

* * *

Just now—a wren trumpets its triplet song.
The sun pours in. Radiance
in the wingspread of the ruby—throated

haloing the daylilies'
clean yellow, in their green stems penciled
on the light—

and then restless waking, the ache
of words incomplete in their praise.

from *Against Consolation* (2001)

Self-Portrait

So strongly present, enclosed
in familiar features: all you
ever see, your self, unreal
to the Buddhist monk, but
something you cannot get rid of.

Inconceivable, this face, yours
just once to wear, that says, *You
can go this far and no further.*
That grins, self-mockingly,
when you try to reach with words'

tenuous liaisons what you believe
words do not invent.
Your petitions repeat themselves,
endlessly trying to get it right,
but still you hear only

your own voice, your will
never strong enough
to will nothing. So here
you are, fleshed out in features
that tell the same old story

year after year, the end
just beginning to make itself
clear in the bony ridges
rising to the surface
of your cheeks, in the deep

holes into which your eyes
stare, and sink, an emptiness
asking, *What have you ever seen
beyond the point of vanishing
to which we have brought you?*

Questions

I often watched you praying, amazed
by how your mind righted itself
as you spoke, the broken world collected
in your murmuring voice, in words
which found the path through the maze
of disconnections your brain had become,

and asked myself whether your mind
(so much already stricken from memory)
fixed on easy rote requirements;
or if those words were the impress of God's
burning seal, your mind long given
to the relinquishments of prayer; or if, simply,
the words themselves were what you held to,
whatever world was left, living and meaning in them.

Nests

More than we imagined,
visible now that we can see
through the leafless branches—

nests, in the lilacs, near
the trunk of a weeping cherry,
on a maple branch horizon.

In them, the past
summer: dead grasses,
milkweed and dandelion

down, our lost cat's
white fur, line I cut
from a fishing reel, bits

of scattered fingernail-
sized eggshells—a robin's
pale blue and, the color

of century-old photographs,
with spots of two shades
of brown on cream, the remains

of a phoebe's eggs. Over
seven days in June, 1855,
Thoreau filled a journal

with quick jottings on tens
of nests—date, place,
type—as he tried to teach

his eyes to *saunter,* to celebrate
without ordering what was
gathered from odds and ends

and sown here and there
like the random matter of creation.
We try, too, but find ourselves

looking at these nests as if they
were old letters or diaries
that conceal as much as they

confide about a world
scattered with bits of narrative,
a story we cannot quite tell

and cannot keep from telling.

Gift

    How carefully he unwrapped it
from his handkerchief—as if it were a relic
    and not the skull-bone

    of a Florida sailcat, a sham
trinket for tourists who'd like a story to tell,
    another legend of the true

    cross or of a world revealing
itself in signs that say there's always something
    underneath: boil the catfish's

    thin sill of flesh away
and the reticulate bone beneath is revealed
    as the crucifix it was meant to be.

    Shake the cross, and hear
the storied dice cast for Christ's garments.
    At first glance, I saw the cross,

    even the body hanging there,
outstretched. But where the loving face
    of Christ should have been

    there was only some bony
voodoo conjunction of a ram's curled horns,
    an alligator's toothy grin—

    a sign, I guess, truer
to a world grotesque with human misery,
    where, as Flannery O'Connor

    said about the deformed half
of everyone, the good in us is always half-

      completed and under

      construction. Of course,
it's not a sign at all— just a junkshop curio,
      a cross of fishbone I've kept

      for years on the mantle
in my study. I'm learning slowly to admire it
      for what it is: a stripped-down

      bone curved where the brain's
blueprint of fluid motions once was harbored;
      a network of beautifully

      dovetailing pieces created by
chance and function which, when it's taken up,
      has the cool patience of a shell,

      the ocean's raw, clean smell.
If it says anything at all by not speaking,
      it's *fix your eyes on finitude,*

      the only path to wholeness—it is
      what has been given to you.

Against Consolation

    The lecturer is talking
about Weil's essay on "Detachment."
    The scent of lilacs
intoxicates the air inside the room,

    cut branches brought in
to represent the flowering outside,
    spring flaring up
again like those beliefs, I imagine,

    Weil warns against—
beliefs which fill up voids and sweeten
    what is bitter. A thousand
miles from here, you have given up

    belief in the providential
ordering of events. No proverb sweetens
    your suffering. What endures
is your bewilderment—the freakish

    wheel of that truck
breaking off and hurtling through
    the sunlit air, not enough
time to say *Look out* or even *Shit,*

    before it struck
your car, one of hundreds lined up
    in rush-hour traffic
on the other side of the highway.

    You told me, the more
you think, the less you understand.
    You can't explain
the roof caved in all around you,

    your two friends buried
under metal, and you, who sat alongside
    them, untouched.
Home from the hospital, your friends

    dead, you went to
the kitchen, and everything, you said,
    was just as you left it,
as if the accident were only an interruption

    in daily life, a tornado
that leaves a kitchen table set for dinner.
    The contradictions the mind
comes up against—these are the only realities:

    they are the criterion
of the real. Weil again, who believes,
    we come to know
our *radical contingency* only through

    such contradictions.
We must suffer them unconsoled.
    Let the accident go,
your friends tell you, *Don't hold on—*

    what we say, I fear,
to rid ourselves of the pain we feel
    when your pain closes
in on us. It's late in the afternoon

    and the rustling
of feet and papers has begun. I look out
    the window—a gusty wind
polishes the morning's rain-washed glass

    of air, and the late sun
lavishes each new green with its shine.

I'd like to dismiss Weil's
haunted, unnerving life as my colleague

   quickly does, the lecture
ended: "Brilliant, but crazy." Anorexic,
     psychotic, suicidal. Labels
that fit, I suppose, and yet I cannot deny

   the stark attraction
of her words. *Stay with your suffering,*
     I've heard her say
over and over today, always the extremist.

   The last time I saw you,
I knew you lived at the border of what is
     bearable, that you'd seen
the skeleton underneath all your thought,

   everything stripped
of sense or summation; you knew
     your friend's deaths
would make no more sense in time

   and you would have
to live in that knowledge—no, not
     knowledge, the word
itself a kind of consolation, but the void

   Weil speaks of,
where you cannot escape the skewed
     wheel of a truck, the blood
on your hands, the voice you still have

   that calls out, *O God, no,*
the scent of lilacs that pierces the air
     each spring for no cause,
beautifully innocent of meaning.

Gratitude

In his prison letters, Bonhoeffer is thankful
for a hairbrush, for a pipe and tobacco,
for cigarettes and Schelling's *Morals* Vol. II.
Thankful for stain remover, laxatives,
collar studs, bottled fruit and cooling salts.
For his Bible and hymns praising what is
fearful, which he sings, pacing in circles
for exercise, to his cell walls where he's hung
a reproduction of Durer's *Apocalypse*.
He's thankful for letters from his parents
and friends that lead him back home,
and for the pain of memory's arrival,
his orderly room of books and prints too far
from the nightly sobs of a prisoner
in the next cell whom Bonhoeffer does not know
how to comfort, though he believes religion
begins with a neighbor who is within reach.
He's thankful for the few hours outside
in the prison yard, and for the half-strangled
laughter between inmates as they sit together
under a chestnut tree. He's thankful even
for a small ant hill, and for the ants that are
all purpose and clear decision. For the two
lime trees that mumble audibly with the workings
of bees in June and especially for the warm
laying on of sun that tells him he's a man
created of earth and not of air and thoughts.
He's thankful for minutes when his reading
and writing fill up the emptiness of time,
and for those moments when he sees himself
as a small figure in a vast, unrolling scroll,
though mostly he looks out over the plains
of ignorance inside himself. And for that,
too, he's thankful: for the self who asks,

Who am I?—the man who steps cheerfully
from this cell and speaks easily to his jailers,
or the man who is restless and trembling
with anger and despair as cities burn and Jews
are herded into railroad cars—can
without an answer, say finally, *I am thine,*
to a God who lives each day,
as Bonhoeffer must, in the knowledge
of what has been done, is still being done,
his gift a refusal to leave his suffering, for which,
even as the rope is placed around his neck
and pulled tight, Bonhoeffer is utterly grateful.

Kafka and the Rabbi of Belz

Rain for days and rain again tonight,
but the Rabbi's followers have taken to heart
a moment three days back when the Rabbi
emerged for his daily exercise and the rain halted
and the sun, as stories already have it, blazed again.
Kafka has tagged along, invited by a friend
who has told him how, when the Rabbi speaks,
everyday objects take on subtler forms.

By the swollen river, the Rabbi stares
so intently at the moving water, Kafka's friend
feels the Rabbi transferring the world into himself.
Kafka watches a swan that never once turns
its head, the bird utterly complete in itself,
inconvertible. It glitters in a circle of lamplight
then disappears under a stone bridge, an interval
passing so quickly it might never have been.

Gusts of wind make the flames in the gaslights
spurt and sputter as if any one of them, or all,
might break into speech. Dead leaves stir
from their piles and are lifted, weightless and figured
for a moment, before dropping to the rain-pocked
street. Above, the trees gesture mutely. The Rabbi
invokes Ezekiel, God's breath entering the bones
of the dead so that they stand up, alive again.

Kafka tells his friend the leaves are just leaves,
and this is quite enough for him.
On the walk back, Kafka sickens himself
with thoughts of work he should be doing,
has not done. When he looks down
the empty streets smeared with rain, the city

appears, as if through the wrong end
of a telescope, to be shrunken and abandoned.

A few days later, to his friend's bewilderment
and surprise, Kafka returns to follow behind
the Rabbi and his students. As they walk,
the sun dissolving over Belz grants
the streets and buildings another, brighter life,
every edge gleaming. The Rabbi is talking
of what is sacred in every human being—
the sense, despite all odds, that life itself is good.

Kafka finds himself recalling a single paragraph
he wrote over and over, how it shone
unexpectedly with what he could not say,
the words enlarged, it seemed, by what was
uninterpretable, defiantly other, yet
requiring words. When his friend asks why
he has come, Kafka shakes his head and says,
there is always something unaccounted for.

Moths

I woke to the flutter of all
their wings over the screen
as, slowly, they assembled
themselves out of the dusty
half-light of morning—
thirty-four moths,
their small grey-brown bodies
covering the screen like lichen.
At noon, they basked
in what little sun there was,
the pale September light
resting briefly on wings
that moved hardly at all
yet never stopped moving
until the moths began
to die. Even then they
seemed more composed
than exhausted, taking
the time they needed,
as if they were dreaming
their death into being.
They simply became their end,
death so naturally wrought,
I needed to touch each one
to be certain. Where
I placed my finger, they broke
out of their bodies
in little puffs of dust, leaving
behind an imprint
on the screen. By then
evening had entered
the day, and the sky, dense
with saturated colors,
collapsed in on itself,

the low clouds igniting
in a bonfire of last light.
And I felt suddenly
the slow, irreversible moment-
to-moment urgency
of every thing to keep
moving— and I leaned close
to the screen and blew
on what remained
until nothing was there,
then stood a while listening
to the wind in the leaves
while the plush dark freed
a scattering of stars and the moon
broke clear of the trees.

Sam Cooke: _Touch the Hem of His Garment_

    As if he cannot help himself
from adding up what's lost to the good times
    so difficult to have in this world,

    Cooke's throaty voice warbles
up out of his reed-thin, man-child body,
    half-balm, half aching need,

    his trademark whoa-ooh-oh-oh-oh
lingered over, drawn out until it hangs in air,
    honey-tongued, heavenly, fragile

    as consolation. I'm listening
to a 1956 recording, and Cooke, twenty-five,
    has already discovered his gift

    for making women tremble
and shake with the spirit in church aisles.
    He's retelling the Gospel story

    of a woman who wants only
to touch the hem of Christ's robe, a song
    that will sell twenty-five thousand copies,

    propel Cooke into a gospel star,
and begin the long chain of small decisions
    that ends with a bullet in his lungs.

    Still eight years away—
the $3-and-up motel, the hooker charging
    assault, Cooke's cherry red Ferrari

   purring in the parking lot
as he slumps to the floor, naked save for
   an overcoat and one expensive shoe—

   but I can't keep from hearing
the urgency in his voice as the woman, pushed
   by the terror of self-recognition,

   her flesh dying from the inside
out, staggers through the crowd around Jesus,
   and, with only the slightest brush

   of her fingers, touches
his robe, believing it will make her whole.
   Who has touched me? Jesus asks,

   and Cooke sings, *It was I-I-I*,
extending the moment in his clear, sustained
   yodel, pulling us into the miracle

   of how, after night-long drifts
from bar to bar, the slur of zippers and
   whiskeyed words dimming the nameless

   landscapes of a hundred
identical blackened factories stuck between
   billboards and railway bridges,

   after a week of days piling
one on another like dirty laundry, Sunday arrives,
   and everyone rises and testifies

   and sways under the wings
of notes that swoop and glide and make us whole,
   if only for the duration of the song.

Pause

    (for Robert)

A teenager now, already it's hard
for you to feel more than the practiced
ironies and diffidence, too many
hours already spent pretending
you've seen it all, and repeatedly.

An hour ago, I dropped a book
and it fell open to this—*only chance
can speak to us*. I thought of Picasso,
of how he found his sculpture of a bull
in the odd conjunctions of a rubbish heap,

an old bicycle seat lying near
a rusted handlebar becoming the bull's
head. I don't know if chance spoke
to Picasso, or why thinking of that
happy accident led me to the night

you were born. Your mother's water
had broken and, driven by worry,
the hospital two hours off, the road
fogged-in and narrowed to what
our car lights could dimly map,

I almost drove over a baby rabbit,
a distillate of rain and moon-shot fog
that formed suddenly out of mist,
and brought us to a standstill.
Your mother and I just sat there,

forgetting ourselves and where we were,
as slowly, and a little at a time,
the rabbit became solid and actual:
first the alert, twigged ears diamonded
by rain-lit mist at each hair's tip;

then the downy, crescent shaped body
poised on those nimble-muscled feet
created for feints and dartings.
So vulnerable and yet so completely
at ease—only a rabbit, it took all

our attention. As we sat there,
we began to hear what was happening
around us—the sluice-rush of water
in a nearby brook and the fainter
background simmering of raindrops

in a fuchsia hedge touched by wind.
Even a dog barking and the ping
of rain on the car's metal roof
seemed a completely new language.
I can't explain why one incident

triggers another or why, together,
they become something else entirely.
I'd like to call it the plenitude of
the unintended. The truth is,
I don't know if chance speaks or if

the mind just cobbles together whatever
it needs—but this world is full of
accidental moments that can stop us
in our tracks and wake in us again
the strangeness we were born to.

from *Common Life* (2006)

A Prayer to Adam

Muse of names,
help us to know
what we cannot name.

Gardener of paradise,
help us grow upright
with the modesty

of plants that find
freedom in their lack
of choices, and thrive.

Father of death,
help us to live
with our dying

so that we may find
ourselves walking back
down a path we forgot,

towards a field
here on earth
where the sun is

so bright and clear
even the dullest sparrow
is seen in the richness

of its browns and grays,
the streaks on its breast
numbered in our sight.

Luther and the Devil

> When I began to lecture on the Psalms and I was sitting
> in the refectory after we had sung matins, studying and
> writing my notes, the Devil came and thudded three times
> in the storage chamber as if dragging a bushel away.

Someone once remarked the medieval air
was so thick with demons, a needle dropped
randomly from heaven would have to pierce
one or two on its way down. These days
we're more likely to believe in poltergeists
than the heavy-footed, skulking Adversary
who shows up in Luther's little story.

Now, when Milton's Satan of *obdurate pride
and stedfast hate* can be understood in terms
of sibling rivalry, how quaint that path
through the Psalms seems; likewise, the soul
disturbed by the racket of a jealous Devil
who needs to be wherever God is. Who believes
that figure of a bushel being dragged away?

Yet we catch certainly a glimmer of Luther's
pain over the sure step gone astray,
the barbed hours to come when nothing satisfies,
when that dull thudding in the storage chamber
seems everywhere, centerless, and there is
no escape from the tightly spiralled Nautilus
of the self that endures by choosing blindly.

And so perhaps we can come to understand again
why, when Luther turns back to the Psalms
and his writing, he looks hard for the Devil
harbored in his words, having learned too often

how that old Adversary shows up each time
the soul comes close to letting itself be found,
his soft mouth whispering one more illusory solace.

Peregrine Falcon, New York City

On the 65th floor where he wrote
advertising copy, joking about
the erotic thrall of words that had
no purpose other than to make
far too many buy far too much,
he stood one afternoon face to face
with a falcon that veered on the blade
of its wings and plummeted, then
swerved to a halt, wings hovering.

An office of computers clicked
behind him. Below, the silence
of the miniature lunch time crowds
and toy-like taxis drifting without
resolve to the will of others.
This bird's been brought in, he thought,
*to clean up the city's dirty problems
of too many pigeons. It's a hired beak.*

Still he remained at the tinted glass
windows, watching as the falcon
gave with such purpose its self
to the air that carried it, its sheer falls
breaking the mirrored self-reflections
of glass office towers. He chided
himself: *this is how the gods come
to deliver a message or a taunt,*
and, for a moment, the falcon
seemed to wait for his response,
the air articulate with a kind of
wonder and terror. Then it was gone.

He waited at the glass until he felt
the diminishment of whatever

had unsettled him. And though
the thin edge of the falcon's wings
had opened the slightest fissure in him
and he'd wandered far in thought,
he already felt himself turning back
to words for an ad, the falcon's power
surely a fit emblem for something.

Yard Sale

Jumbled on tables and in boxes—
dessert plates painted with strawberries
and rimmed in gold leaf, pottery

bowls, and teapots shaped like a cottage
and a cat; over a dozen stray mugs
bought here and there, no place

we can remember—small things
that spoke of coziness and good cheer.
Along the driveway's edge, a chair

we couldn't find comfort in, a table
of odd clocks and mirrors that caught
an eye for whimsy too whimsically.

Why do these things pain us so?—
each step bringing forward
what we thought we'd put behind:

these long lines of shoes like refugees
too easily exiled to closets
after an aching week of remorse

and self-chastisement; a menagerie
of hats that once seemed so jaunty,
so rife with adventure; so many ties,

their quick tug and dazzle matching
a need to buy *something*
after all those hours at the mall.

And here, on a small island of grass,
those castaway skirts and pants

bought in the bright reflection

of store mirrors. Everywhere,
another history of who we were
or are: piles of unread books;

records and CDs which, listened to,
turned out, inevitably, not to be
what was desired; a first solid state

amplifier, a first CD player,
ever-larger television sets, screens
dark with vacant introspection.

And scattered on the sunlit grass,
glittering like the toys of children
whose attention soon waned,

a tread mill and weight set, tennis
racquets, golf clubs, and a pair of skis
lying like the hands of a clock.

Hours gone, no buyers in sight,
we wonder if anyone has seen the signs
we posted across the river.

A dog barks. We circle aimlessly,
as if our own yard's become a hell
of things we're forced to wander

among, each object something we have
no use for, a ghostly reminder
of the life we never gave to it,

a history of what did not happen
the way we meant it to and now,
unwittingly, a history we cannot escape.

Visitations

It's an old story. This is how it begins.
In a grotto outside a church the air trembles
and a statue of Mary begins to weep tears

of blood from her bright blue eyes.
In a few days a crowd grows, like exiles
returning to their homeland. A man says

Mary spoke to him, telling him the earth
is a vast catacomb of tombs, a planet of death.
Another can suddenly see. A woman dreams

that her heart is a great tree beginning to bud
after a hard winter. A CAT scan reveals the tears
are really blood— a DNA test, the blood is male.

A scientist says the shadow of an ancient belief
wants to be truth again; a priest how deep
in us lies the longing to touch the sacred.

The story goes on being told, like a prayer
prayed ceaselessly to keep a path open to God.
Though Mary has stopped weeping,

two men vault a temporary barrier protecting
the statue and sheer off one of her hands,
an entire side of her face with an iron bar.

When questioned they say, *now she reflects
the world as it is*—godless and damaged.
This is how the story ends without ending:

The men are arrested, security is doubled.
The lack of new tears from the plaster statue

sends many off to see a face that has appeared

on the side of a barn two towns away.
There are other reports of her—a woman's
kneeling shape traced in the cracks of a plaster wall;

a mantled form discovered in a tree halved by
lightning—as if, because Mary is no longer here,
she is again being found everywhere.

At the grotto, the sky simply returns to being
the sky. So too the sun and grass. And Mary
goes back to looking over the world

with her one good eye which does not weep
but has the haunting calm of a Buddha
who has seen everything and accepts.

Sanctuary

The story goes that there were *promptings*
one night, voices, rising from the river,
speaking in the trees, and that he, Salvatore,
of North Main Street, Willimantic,
halfway through the darkness of his life, knew
immediately the task that lay before him.

He saw seven hills and seven terraces
inside the rutted incline choked with sumac
behind his house. He carved steps
into the earth, and sowed his terraces
with iron bathtubs stood on end, each becoming
a small grotto, a shelter for plaster St. Teresas,

St. Johns, Marys in need of blue paint,
and of course, St. Anthony, restorer of lost things.
And Salvatore, generous, artless, a collector
of all those things that were never good enough,
knew the uncanny freedom of the self-forgetful
as he went about his work. His New Jerusalem

always under construction lay among the patchwork
neighborhood of crimped houses noisy with crying
and bills to pay, of scuffed yards and sooty trees.
Those who visited his grotto sometimes said
that, as they sat there watching the river glide
below, the smallness and stinginess they carried

inside drifted away. But it was only a matter of time
before Salvatore spent what little he had
on what little he could make. Twenty years
after he began, aged and sickly, more than half-crazy
with his mission, he was placed in a nursing home,
his *Sanctuary of Love* sold off piecemeal for back taxes.

Pictures in the local papers showed happy bidders
leaving with armfuls of saints. There was one
picture of the younger Salvatore standing, shirtsleeves
rolled, in front of a first upright tub as if he were
the figure being placed inside it: an ordinary man
who knew all he needed to know about the life ahead.

Hummingbird Annunciation

It's no wonder Gabriel appears
at my elbow, flashing his ruby throat, levitating,
and holding steady a foot or so
from a blooming orange azalea. It's not me
he wants but those trumpeting petals.

Earlier this morning, I looked at a book
of annunciation paintings, the curve
of Mary's body finding a graceful equipoise
between fear and acceptance as she holds herself
open to the awful wonder of an angel

who tells her the good news
but also that her child's silent partner
will be death. Perhaps all annunciations
involve the infernal terms living asks of us all.
My dear friend must decide today

whether her husband of forty years should be
removed from life support. She gave herself
to the next thing that needed doing
when her husband's slow, terrible dying
became unredeemable. And me?

I've often shrunk the world to my desire
that everything will be all right,
a crude defense meant to exclude whatever
is uncontrollable. I turn away, afraid to be
empty enough for something to enter.

Except perhaps something as small
as this tiny whirlwind, this sheen
of emerald and ruby darting in and out
of blooms, buzzing at my elbow as if with news
I can choose or not choose to hear.

Rosary Bead, Netherlands, c. 1500

It asks to be handled and touched,
this two inch elaborately carved
sphere of boxwood cloistered inside
a glass case. For an hour now
I've tried to see it with the eyes of
the Abbess who would have held it
closed in her fingers, and traced
its equatorial crown of thorns
where it has been hinged to open
on an interior storied world

hidden behind two carved doors
upon which Adam and Eve concede to
their blurred, competing desires.
Hail Mary, full of grace...
Inside, more than a hundred
figures, fractions of an inch long,
were carved and fitted together
into upper and lower scenes by
a craftsman graced with patience
and the belief, perhaps, that inside

the emptiness of a hollowed out
sphere of wood, a whole creation
could take place—birth, death,
and the life between made visible,
a narrative in which someone
might come to know herself—
my nun, for instance,
whom I've imagined drawing
Our father, who art in Heaven...
into her mouth, bringing breath

and tongue together, forming
those hovering words again and
again, waiting for that shuddering
emptiness beneath the rote
and homiletic, that ache of relief
that comes when she is rapt
in conversation with a voice that is
her own and not her own,
and which does not speak so much
as fill an absence, and usher in
an odd uncanny calm.
Standing here, I almost feel
the thousands of prayers
that passed her lips and the peace
of saying *Glory be to God the Father* . . .
—almost feel the weight
of this boxwood bead
in my hand, though it remains
behind glass, a beautifully detailed
museum piece from Brabant.

Parable of the Moth

Consider this: a moth flies into a man's ear
one ordinary evening of unnoticed pleasures.
When the moth beats its wings, all the winds
of earth gather in his ear, roar like nothing
he has ever heard. He shakes and shakes
his head, has his wife dig deep into his ear
with a Q-tip, but the roar will not cease.
It seems as if all the doors and windows
of his house have blown away at once—
the strange play of circumstances over which
he never had control, but which he could ignore
until the evening disappeared as if he had
never lived it. His body no longer
seems his own; he screams in pain to drown
out the wind inside his ear, and curses God,
who, hours ago, was a benign generalization
in a world going along well enough.

On the way to the hospital, his wife stops
the car, tells her husband to get out,
to sit in the grass. There are no car lights,
no streetlights, no moon. She takes
a flashlight from the glove compartment
and holds it beside his ear and, unbelievably,
the moth flies towards the light. His eyes
are wet. He feels as if he's suddenly a pilgrim
on the shore of an unexpected world.
When he lies back in the grass, he is a boy
again. His wife is shining the flashlight
into the sky and there is only the silence
he has never heard, and the small road
of light going somewhere he has never been.

Talking Through a Storm

(for Sydney Lea)

Nothing in the sky shows through
the heat-tented dark but auroras
of still distant lightning that open
a path to the pond and fields

below your second story screened-in
porch where we sit after dinner, hoping
to build a world in good conversation.
Thunder builds in this Vermont valley

where, for five windless ninety-plus days,
moisture-ridden air has been shoveled in
from the south and tamped down.
A small wind whispers the rumor of

a cold front as it pushes through
the stale air. We lay our foundation
around family and friends, around
the little rash promises we make over

and over to hold off what we know
is always threatening to shatter. And count
our blessings—the disarming joy of being
loved, the bounty of the natural world

that still takes our sight beyond ourselves.
We're warming up for what it means to be
a poet in an age that doesn't believe
(where we always head) in much beside

the individual's private wanderings in
a world of accidents in which we're one.
But we never arrive, your talk shifting
to a spate of killings in this green kingdom

of spare white frame churches, a county
courthouse, a commons, and two hundred year
old houses. It's the utter contempt for life
that gets you, the trivial reasons that lie

behind driving a sharpened foot-long knife
into the eyes and skull of a local shop owner—
I needed some money for a car payment
the seventeen year old killer said as though

no one could question such necessity.
The others, no more understandable—
a foster mother punched and stabbed
because one of her teenagers couldn't listen

to *that British voice* any longer; a mother shot
by a son who wanted the car keys; a couple,
stabbed in their own study with a Seal 2000
combat knife ordered over the Internet

by two teenagers who wanted to know
what killing someone felt like—
and all within a small radius of where we sit,
the wind picking up as if on cue, the trees

electrified by flares of lightning closing in.
*No shaved head, tattooed Neo-Nazis—
just plain kids, like yours or mine,* you say,
who take no pleasure in being alive,

who look out on the same world as you and I,
and see nothing. A quick sizzle of rain against
the screen, and then the old abandonment—
the wind opening a wide avenue of rain

that pocks the pond, and lacquers the roof
above our heads. Searing headstrong lightning
falls from the sky like some ancient god's
revenge. It splits the dark wide open,

singling out a border oak for its revelation.
For a while we let the thunder and rain
become our conversation. I wonder
if those teenagers might even hate these sounds

I love—the silvery whoosh of cold wind,
the different percussions of rain on wood, on
metal, thunder ramifying itself in the mountains.
I've seen my own sons move through our fields

with headphones on, as if katydid and phoebe,
the keening call of a redtail, had long been
stripped of any meaning. A north wind
rouses the trees, blows the ground fog away

above the steaming grass. Clouds are
streaming overhead, backlit by an unseen
moon. The rain has passed. You say,
these teenage boys talk about their violence

as if it were an act of faith. I suspect it is—
faith in fury, in the demons that drive
the day beyond the small shitty drama
they see as their life. That old bargain

which can't be broken once it's made.
All I can muster is, *they'll spend nearly all
their lives in jail* in a voice caught somewhere
between regret for so much loss so early on,

and my revulsion for what they did.
Then, though it's hate I want to feel for
their cold contempt, or to escape my own
confusion, I find myself telling you a story,

an old rabbinic parable. There's a murder
within the city walls. Who the killer is
seems less important than what every citizen
must do: come to the synagogue and pray

for forgiveness. That old question:
What made the killer hate enough to kill?
What made those ordinary teenagers hate
is beyond our knowing, though we know,

if only in part, the never-satisfied appetite
of evil. We, too, must pray if, for no other reason,
those boys never felt the grace of living—
no matter how we stumble and knock about—

in a world where love is possible,
and the whole entire lot of us has somehow
been kept from our own destruction,
if only barely. But now your children

have wandered in to say goodnight.
I watch you wrap your arms around them,
and lavish them with kisses again and again,
as if each night you are reminded of how close

you came to your own destruction. You hold
them up and look at them, each in turn,
the way you might have looked at them
at birth, singling them out as your own,

as God was said to single out his people.
And then they're off to bed, and we stroll
outside across the wet grass, breathing in
the freshened air. Behind the thinning clouds

are stars, and behind the stars, more stars.
A screech owl in the distance makes its almost
human cry. Raindrops tremble in the trees.
We talk about tomorrow—how the sky will roof

the air above our heads in a clear, washed blue,
and the grass will be greener—though neither
of us can forget those boys who will wake inside
their gray walls, still in a world where nothing matters.

Christmas Soccer Game, 1915

I suppose what made it possible
was that no one expected more
than a day of unhurried hours, better
food, some free time to reread old letters,
write new ones. Small Christmas trees
with candles lined both sides of the trenches
and marked the two days' truce.

Who can explain it?—one minute troops
are sitting in mud, the next raising themselves
out of the trenches, as if all they needed
was a soccer ball to remind them
of who they were. Imagine a Scotsman
heading the ball into the air and catching it
on his instep, then flicking it across

the frosted grass to a German smoking
a cigarette who smiles and settles the ball,
then boots it back. Soon a few soldiers
from both sides circle around the Scotsman
and the ball moves quickly back and forth,
left foot, right foot, all of the men rocking
from side to side, the ball, the cold,

making good neighbors of them all.
A game's begun, a real match without referees,
attack and counterattacks, the ball crossing
from side to side, a match played,
we can imagine, as if it were all that mattered,
as if the game's sudden fizzes of beauty—
three crisp passes or two perfect triangles

lying end to end and pointing to the goal—
could erase what they had learned

to live with. Laughing, out of breath, dizzy
with the speed of the ball skipping over
the frozen earth, did they recognize themselves
for a short while in each other? History says
only that they exchanged chocolate and cigarettes,

relaxed in the last ransomed sunlight.
When the night came and they had retreated
to their own sides, some of the men
wrote about the soccer game as if they had to
ensure the day had really happened. It did.
We have the letters, though none of them say
how, in the next short hours, they needed,

for their own well-being, to forget everything
that had happened that Christmas day.
It was cold, the long rows of candles must have
seemed so small in the dark. Restless, awake
in the trenches, the men, I suppose,
already knew what tomorrow would bring,
how it would be judged by the lost and missing.

My Uncle's Parrot

It's the voice I hear, the one that comes
when my talk suddenly becomes preachy,
and my class of freshmen begin to nod
their heads in assent as I'm delivering
some grand moral claim for Wordsworth's
leech-gatherer, or declaring there is a way
to live out our lives hopeful and happy.

Or it comes when my wife, stepping
from a bath, her neck and belly and legs
diamonded in the bathroom light, stands
before me like some St. Agnes Eve vision,
and I believe that, yes, our bodies are
for climbing that ladder from pleasure
to pleasure upwards to the sublime.

Or when I see on the late night news
how a whole town, businesses included,
turns out to re-erect a block of
tornado-tossed houses and think we could
learn to live in just that state of love,
the beginning of what could be
endlessly multiplying loaves and fish.

Or even when late at night, alone,
reading a good book and listening to
Vivaldi's oboes, a cup of tea warming
my hands, I suddenly think, then and there,
that everything in my life has only had
the illusion of significance, that
the truth is absolute meaninglessness.

At all those times and more, I hear
the point-blank voice of my uncle's parrot

say, *bullshit,* the only word he could
ever teach it, though the parrot possessed
an unerring sense of timing,
a pitch-perfect ear for the exact moment

in the conversation when its shrill trumpet
was required: *bullshit,* it blared again
and again with the authority of a God
who knew, as Pascal said, how to keep faith
and doubt off balance as he went on
balancing both sides of every equation.

Lenten Stanzas

I.

And how should I wait? Should I list
my transgressions—I was cruel, I lied, I let

anger overtake me, I said I knew when I did not.
I turned away too quickly.

And how should I pray? Should I follow him,
who Luke tells us, *being in agony, prayed more earnestly.*

How can I keep myself from distraction?
Can I keep watch any better than his closest friends,

who, each time, woke more eager to do what was needed,
each time more shocked to find their bodies

capable of such betrayal. How can I live in this story
that requires of me what I most want to forget?

II.

When she lifted her eyes I could see
the lesions of her pain, could see the invisible

torment lodged in her like a piece of glass. Anger
and confusion condensed in her tears. No sleep relieved

what happened in her sleep. A man took her,
anonymously, indifferently, completely.

Sometimes she wakes, she said, the night half gone,
and thinks there is only the morning to come.

I could taste the bitterness of what had died in her
as we sat through the afternoon's shadowy light.

Outside, the rain did not wash anything clear.
I had no rosary of words to take away her pain.

III.

And what am I waiting for?
The days come, and the nights. Without refreshment.

IV.

Nothing could be more real than that which makes no sense: what she
said one afternoon. The late March sun was drilling holes in the last
piles of dirty snow. Even through the windows we could feel its heat,
the simple astonishing fact of the earth turning in its direction. She
said she had stopped asking *why her*, had stopped thinking she must
have done something to deserve what had happened. Her cross, she
said, was to shoulder what would never make sense. She needed to
say these things; the light helped. We both knew that what she said
was right and yet knowing so was only the beginning of a different
darkness.

V.

Out of the slow, mournful clarinet comes the Abyss
of the Birds, Messiaen's third movement

which does not move forward so much as pulse
in place, a turning around and around,

like the sad tedium of time we live in and cannot
escape. I am listening to his *Quartet for the End*

of Time, waiting for the clarinet to become a bird,
to quicken like our desire for light, for song.

This morning, the day still dark, a phoebe's
quiescent song caught my attention and kept it.

fee-be, fee-be. Just those two notes over and over
like the simplest *Kyrie* breathed out in the darkness.

VI.

Each candle has been snuffed out. From the darkest
corner of the church, a tenor sings, *Were you there
when they crucified my Lord?* Just that unaccompanied

voice, and the watery shadows, and the lights of a car
splashed against the dark walls and then the voice again,
breaking as it moans those *O, O, O, O's* that cause us

to tremble. What I see in the dark: the necessity
of my staying there. How often I've hurried

towards the sunlit world and my own undoing.
Here, I remember how slowly she lifted her face,

how the words fell from her mouth, how the day darkened
around her. I remember the last time we spoke,

and how she made the past newly present, her pain quivering,
alive again, as if she'd learned such remembrance was

the terrifying terms of any future hope. And now I pray
more earnestly for the strength to wait here in the dark.

Skellig Michael

We have our various reasons: five boatloads of us—
Europeans, Americans, Japanese; birders, photographers,
even modern pilgrims—looking, I suppose,

for something a little out-of-the-way, a little more
than the ordinary next stop on the Ring of Kerry,
looking, perhaps, for the holy in places where it was once

said to be. Eight miles out, the solitary rocks rise
straight out of the sea as if they were giving birth
to themselves. No music here but the screams of

thousands of gannets, shearwaters, kittiwakes and gulls,
the tireless crash and fallback of water breaking itself
apart and reforming along the sheer rock faces.

We've come to climb the steps—600 in all, some
hand-hewn in the stone—to the monastic ruins, lately
reconstructed, like Christianity after the moment

of presence had passed. The path is steep, then steeper,
the monks' cells nearly 700 feet above the sea. The monks
are long gone, the scene here still as "solemn and sad"

as Lord Dunraven's party of archaeologists found it
at the end of the 19th century. "None should enter here
but the pilgrim and the penitent," the Lord warned.

**

I stop half way up for a breather, and turn to the puffins
lining every ledge. My bird book gives *Fratercula*
as their Latin name. Clown-faced, stubby-tailed, stiff

upright walk—these Little Brothers bring some comic relief
to the tragic feel of this place. They clasp their feet
together prayerfully when they take off and fly, though *fly*

is too strong a word. An elongated hop comes closer
to the truth. They must have given their hermit brothers,
even in the most dispiriting of times, a good laugh.

How hard, that choice the monks often faced:
to starve themselves or club to death the puffy chicks,
their one source of food when the sea and the few

arable patches of dirt could not provide. The wind
never ceases here. Its voice everywhere, ventriloquial,
one moment it speaks in the Spirit's comforting tones,

the next in devilish harangues tongued through
pocked and pitted stone. In this place nothing is ever
one thing and only one thing: wind, birds, stone, ocean.

**

I suspect (who can keep from reading his own life
into others?) these hermit monks thought this beautiful,
forsaken island was just far enough away from everything

to approach themselves. Even the cleverest among them
must have run quickly through the self's retinue of tricks
in this stony, treeless place and come to the cliff face

inside himself and the sheer drop below. *One who is
not alone*, Philoxenos said, *has not yet discovered
his identity.* The ocean stretches below like some vast,

unknowable deity made manifest in an endless supply
of unraveling waves. I'm up on my feet again, approaching
Christ's Saddle, the name for the steepest incline before

a stone cross marks the gate of the little monastery.
In the past, the sinful climbed these steps again and again
as a public penance. I'm looking to feel the stern

reductions of wind and water. Inside the gate,
I duck and enter a monk's 8x8 windowless cell,
waiting in the darkness for things to come clear.

**

I can hear chips of bird song, see, through the door,
a small rectangle of fast-graying sky. So much
undoing must have been done here. So much to give up—

the hands of a mother, a father's voice, the slow touch
of a woman, the news and gossip of the world. How long
it takes, how hard it is to see oneself. More than half

my life already over, I have come to know lately
how little I know, and how even that gets in my way,
my mind trafficking in perfectly managed confusions,

in creating comfort and security where neither truly exist.
I've kept myself from facing what Philoxenos saw:
the unreality of the self. I don't know what these monks

came to know. Chances are, for all their privations,
they were never filled with more than their own good
intentions; that, most days, there was only silence

and the wide and terrible emptiness of the stars
shimmering on the depths of the ocean. Yet it's possible
that this barest of places stripped them of all those

hopeless explanations that are never good enough
to explain the origins of evil, or why the truly innocent
suffer so much more than anyone could ever deserve.

Perhaps, as they went about celebrating mass, planting,
fishing, climbing up and down to the sea, they sometimes
stopped to listen to a storm-tossed chaffinch and felt

its song inside themselves and, in that moment,
celebrated its gratuity and the unexpected plenitude
that could create itself out of their stony emptiness.

**

I've come to their small graveyard of stone crosses,
each of their lives an eye-blink as they knew. I'd like to
kneel down and touch my forehead to the stone

as they might have done before their simple altar—
some act to honor the gravity of what they tried
to do. But too many other tourists are nearby.

I'll walk instead to the site of a hermit who lived on
the other side, apart even from his brothers here.
I've read there's a shelf of eroded rock with a hole

in it called the Needle's Eye. About the size of a man,
it extends out over a rocky cove, an open ocean
of wind-driven waves threshing stones 600 feet below.

For what it's worth, I'll lie down on the rock
as so many others before me have, and think of
just how soon we pass through, poor at last.

Advent Stanzas

I.

Are we always creating you, as Rilke said,
trying, on our best days,
to make possible your coming-into-existence?

Or are you merely a story told in the dark,
a child's drawing of barn and star?

Each year you are born again. It is no remedy

for what we go on doing to each other,
for history's blind repetitions of hate and reprisal.

Here I am again, huddled in hope. For what
do I wait?—I know you only as something missing,
and loved beyond reason.

As a word in my mouth I cannot embody.

II.

On the snow-dusted field this morning—an etching
of mouse tracks declares the frenzy of its hunger.

The plodding dawn sun rises to another day's
one warm hour. I'm walking to the iced-in local pond

where my neighbors have sat through the night
waiting for something to find their jigged lure.

The sky is paste white. Each bush and tree keeps
its cold counsel. I'm walking head-on into a wind

that forces my breath back into my mouth.
Like rags of black cloth, crows drape a dead oak.

When I pass under them, their cries rip a seam
in the morning. Last week a lifelong friend told me,

There's no such thing as happiness. It's ten years
since he found his son, then a nineteen-year old

of extraordinary grace and goodness, curled up
in his dormitory room, unable to rise, to free

himself of a division that made him manic and
depressed, and still his son struggles from day to day,

the one partial remedy a dismal haze of drugs.
My friend hopes these days for very little—a stretch of

hours, a string of a few days when nothing in his son's life
goes terribly wrong. This is the season of sad stories:

the crippling accident, the layoffs at the factory,
the family without a car, without a house, without money

for presents. The sadder the human drama, the greater
our hope, or so the television news makes it seem

with its soap-opera stories of tragedy followed up
with ones of good will—images of Santas' pots filling up

at the malls, truckloads of presents collected for the shelters,
or the family posed with their special-needs child

in front of a fully equipped van given by the local dealership.
This is the season to keep the less fortunate in sight,

to believe that generosity will be generously repaid.
We've strung colored lights on our houses and trees,

and lit candles in the windows to hold back the dark.
For what do we hope?—That our candles will lead you

to our needs? That your gift of light will light
these darkest nights of the year? That our belief

in our own righteousness will be vindicated?
The prophet Amos knew the burden of your coming.

The day of the Lord is darkness, he said, *darkness, not light,*
as if someone went into a house and rested a hand against a wall,

and was bitten by a snake. Amos knew the shame of
what we fail, over and over, to do, the always burning

image of what might be. Saint Paul, too, saw
the whole creation groaning for redemption.

And will you *intercede with sighs too deep for words*
because you love us in our weakness, because

you love always, suddenly and completely, what is
in front of you, whether it is a lake or leper.

Because you come again and again to destroy the God
we keep making in our own image. Will we learn

to pray: May our hearts be broken open. Will we learn
to prepare a space in which you might come forth,

in which, like a bolt of winter solstice light,
you might enter the opening in the stones, lighting

our dark tumulus from beginning to end?

III.

All last night the tatter of sleet, ice descending,
each tree sheathed in ice, and then, deeper
into the night, the shattering cracks and fall
of branches being pruned by gusts of wind.

It is the first morning after the longest night,
dawn colorless, the sun still cloud-silvered.
Four crows break the early stillness, an apocalypse
of raucous squawks. My miniature four horseman

take and eat whatever they can in the field
outside my door: a deer's leg my dog has dragged
home. Above them, the flinty sun has at last fired
a blue patch of sky, and suddenly each ice-transfigured

tree shines. Each needle of pine, each branch
of ash, throws off sparks of light. Once,
a rabbi saw a spark of goodness trapped inside
each evil, the very source of life for that evil—

a contradiction not to be understood, but suffered,
the rabbi explained, though the one who prays
and studies Torah will be able to release that spark,
and evil, having lost its life-giving source, will cease.

When I finally open my door and walk
into the field, every inch of my skin seems touched
by light. So much light cannot be looked at:
my eyelids slam down like a blind.

All morning I drag limbs into a pile. By noon,
the trees and field have lost their shine. I douse
the pile of wood with gas, and set it aflame,
watching sparks disappear in the sky.

IV.

This is the night we have given for your birth.

After the cherished hymns, the prayers, the story
of the one who will become peacemaker,
healer of the sick, the one who feeds
the hungry and raises the dead,

we light small candles and stand in the dark

of the church, hoping for the peace
a child knows, hoping to forget career, mortgage,
money, hoping even to turn quietly away

from the blind, reductive selves inside us.

We are a picture a child might draw
as we sing *Silent Night, Holy Night.*

Yet, while each of us tries to inhabit the moment
that is passing, you seem to live in-between
the words we fill with our longing.

The time has come
to admit I believe in the simple astonishment
of a newborn.

And also to say plainly, as Pascal knew, that you will live
in agony even to the end of the world,

your will failing to be done on earth
as it is in heaven.

Come, o come Emmanuel,

I am a ghost waiting to be made flesh by love
I am too imperfect to bear.

Sullenness

Why should I open my eyes?—the dark's flush
against the windows, trees inked in, the moon still
disappearing. And yet, undeniably, the day's begun.
No colors, but first rush of cheeps and partial songs,
first sense of light behind the margins of darkness.
Alright, I'm up. Not that it matters. The sun will find
its way over the eastward hills without my help.
By the time I go outside the day has gathered
substance. A breeze shuffles shadows and light
golds and blue-greens under the larches, and the grass
in the field bounces the sun from its billion blades.
It's the 17th of June, a morning of rinsed air
after last night's storm. A phoebe darts out and back
from a dead branch, harvesting insects. I'm getting
myself up each morning to look at these things.
I can't explain why exactly. I confess it's nice
to feel small when the light, pale as a match flame
at first, suddenly catches in the flammable air
and the sky's reds and oranges blaze above my sight's
horizon, and then above the trees. And reading
Dante recently, I felt how narrow my sympathies
were. I didn't see myself wedged in slime,
gurgling the Styx's mud because I'd been sullen
in the sun's sweet air, but I felt again how vestigial,
how wary and flawed with ironies, my instinct
for praise had become. So I'm out here watching
the slow tai chi of the gauzy larches, and listening
to a rooster's faithfulness to the hour, a car starting up,
a dog barking, then being called in, and now
I'm looking again at a border of irises planted years ago,
their deep blue magnifying the sky's blue singleness.
No signs or connections, no common-to-us-all truth.
Just the felicities of each thing-in-itself, and the self
trying to expand its boundaries. I'm not sure

if sullenness was more of a sin when the glories
of God could be seen more easily, but I'm sure
that Dante was right, that each day should open
my mouth in song, and that what I refuse is hell.

Sacraments

(for a twentieth anniversary)

Even just beginning, this June day raises my sights,
the milky sky turning bluer, this breeze that's come
from Canada freshening the air. I'm watching
your hands slice bread for breakfast.
Outside, the falling and rising flight of a goldfinch
and five earthbound robins that scuttle a few paces
then lean their alertness toward grass still at its greenest.

Last night's naked needs are clothed, but I'm remembering
how the taste of you brought your first flavor back
to me, like the taste of many summers in a mouthful of wine.
Whatever worries we've piled up are sidestepped
by a slant of light elaborating the orange of the poppies
when we step outside into this morning's luck
falling from thin air, and catch in each other's eyes

that first Edenic couple who gave each other
a body and a face. Strange how days like this enter us
and are intimate, a conversation with clouds
steeping in the east, with a sky that stretches us
and yet is human-scaled. Stranger still, how easy it is
just now with each other to accept all our errors,
though they cannot be undone, now or ever.

Ode to Ordinariness

I.

Our little ration of things gone right, god of all that is
    too humdrum for our notice, you carry out
your work under our noses, predictable as the weather.
    When I open the door for today's paper,
there you are, unseen as always, in the manic circles
    of a neighbor's setter that tosses a sunny
cloud of goldfinches into the air and gives the giggles
    to a first grader two doors down, waiting
inside this morning's teakettle mist and her father's coat
    covering her shoulders. And now the sky
is turning blue over the city and the yellow bus rolls up
    and the girl disappears in her seat, her father
left waving to a window where the sun flares, suspended
    for a moment while he continues to shout
last minute consolations for both of them: *I'll be waiting*
    in this same spot when you come back at three.

II.

And you're there with the mail, the usual bills and a letter
    from a friend (whose marriage fell apart
a year ago), who writes now about what stays the same:
    Still teaching and writing about X, playing
some decent tennis; with a robin (what else) in the noonday
    sun that scurries a few feet, stops, then tilts
its head and holds steady in the great alertness and purpose
    of its hunger. With the men eating lunch
outside Linemaster Switch who soak up the good will
    of this first warm day of spring and dream
of getting in a little fishing in Maine. And you are in
    a conversation overheard at the supermarket—

Thank God the doctors caught it so soon—and in the face of
    the wife who knew that just this once,
and only for now, her husband had passed through the eye
    of Fate's needle. Our little god of reprieves,
of the breathing spaces between living and dying, between
    disasters and raptures, you grant us the luxury
of your dailiness, the *nothing much* we come to count on.

III.
We praise you: for the safe return of the school bus, for
    everyone home for supper. Praise to recurrence
and status quo, to the sun returning like a second chance
    after this evening's shower, and for sparks
of rain igniting the rooftops of the Rogers Corporation
    where chimney swifts that left with the sun
have come back, soaring and banking now in the evening's
    tints of yellow and orange. And praise for
the moon rising like a clockface and for the small triangle
    of shadowed flesh where I've unbuttoned
my wife's blouse and for the identical feelings I first felt
    leaning to kiss that exact spot twenty years
ago. Praise for these last hours before sleep when we count
    back through the day, and pick up a book
we've read over and over again because each time it is
    so familiar, so strangely different and new.

Pigeon Man

    In retrospect, it all seems so
unlikely, how, every Easter, he'd come again,
    the pigeon man from Rhode Island,
in his old truck full of wooden cages. Gathered

    once already, we'd gather again,
outside the church on the Common. I'd like to
    remember blue skies and sunny Easter hats,
but a whited-out sun and a hem of clouds is closer

    probably to the truth. Or rain.
I can recall the strange mixture of our spirits
    high on resurrection hymns, yet dampened by
nagging reminders—Jim's young wife dying of cancer

    and their two boys who would be
motherless in a month; a divorce of two members
    loved by everyone; a suicide bombing in Jerusalem;
and soldiers occupying the church at Bethlehem.

    Looking back, no year seems free
of grief and suffering, of one sadness or another. Still,
    there were the pigeons. And perhaps a little wind
passing its spirit along the crowns of the Common's maples

    as the pigeon man opened the cages
and sent his flock into the gray sky. They went up as one,
    tumblers, rollers, and tipplers, dozens of them,
turning higher and higher in tight spirals, the undersides

    of their wings refracting whatever light
there was when they spun all at once. They climbed
    straight up above the high school and church,
above the houses on the green, then caught a wind

     and rode it east, out past Putnam
and across the French River, towards Providence,
    becoming a slow-pulsing dot against the cloud cover.
Some of us clapped, some just watched as the flock

     seemed to disappear through a portal
in the clouds, emptiness and fullness held together
    for the moment. Then the pigeon man
gave his tacit nod, climbed into his truck

     and drove home to await his flock.
Impassive as he was, he must have loved the thrill of
    watching his birds fly off and come back,
just as we looked forward yearly to his coming,

     to the pigeons which must have suggested,
whether we believed or not, and even if we knew
    the movement in the opposite direction was far
more common, that grief could suddenly turn to grace.

Lord God Bird

—a nickname for the ivory billed woodpecker

Extinct, though often sighted and pursued
as if you were still of this world; willed
into being, perhaps, by the lost spaces
you inhabit, or because you are part of
a dream we go on dreaming, you recreate
yourself in the moving shadows of gold
and green forest light, and we come close
to understanding why the few who saw you last
cried out, *Lord God!* when the rich carmine
of your crest and the silken black edges
of your wings widened the corridors
between moss hung old-growth cypresses.

Audubon saw you and tried to still the furtive
blurs of your canopied flight in the pose—
upright against a tree he traced for you.
He conceived you as a Van Dyck, those same
radiating qualities of color—arterial red
and veridical whites, the primary yellow
of your eyes fixed against a lapidary black—
and tried to bring you, wholly and life-sized,
to his blank canvas where only the three inch
luminous ivory bill caught you exactly:
a totem which local Indians buried with them
for passage from this world to the next.

And after the great ornithologist Wilson
had wing shot you, and after your cries—
exactly that of a young child—made him fear
for his life, he took you to an inn and asked
for a room for *myself and my baby*. There,

he unwrapped you and felt the grip
of your transformation, those unblinking eyes
that took in that definable world of walls
and a table where he tied you. All the while
he tried to paint you, you hammered a hole
through the plaster and weather boards
of an outside wall. And after he tried to feed

you and after you refused all food and went on
hammering your ivory bill into the table
and the wall for three full days and nights,
as if the fulfilling of that act were the only thing
you could do in the perfection of your birdness,
he watched your wounded, beautiful body
breathe in one very sharp deep breath and die,
and knew, though he could not say why,
that in one exceptional moment of abandon,
you had flown into his imaginings and he could see
you, more completely now that you lay dead,
your red cockade enlivening a depth of dark trees.

Common Life

> *Some even produce at will odorless sounds from*
> *their breech, a kind of singing from the other end.*
> *—(City of God, 14:24)*

Like Christ on the Emmaus road concealed
from his disciples by his ordinariness,
the commonplace is sometimes hardest to see—
so Augustine learned after years of flirting
with a dual world, all those vacillations
between the flesh burying itself in sweetness
like a bee making a heaven of a fallen pear,
and the scrubbed soul set free by
the hair shirt of penitence. In time, he
came to find that his own body, once seen
as a devilish trap predestined for sex,
sickness and death, was a gift, and that even
the lowly worm's *corporeal rotundity* manifested
a harmony of beginning, middle and end
as it inched through the dirt. And so the Good
of creation, which includes the mouth breathing in,
must also include the anus breathing out
its musical flatulence, breaking the silence
between strangers who are reminded of
their common body, as the disciples were that day
when they broke bread after their long walk
with the one they finally knew as their Teacher.

Pentecost in Little Falls, New Jersey

If I arrived early, I had to listen
to hundreds of sewing machines
spiraling their high-pitched arias
up against the mill's metal shell.

Each woman, a soloist withdrawn
into her small cubicle of work,
sang the crazy hope of piecework—
Another zipper, another dollar.

A wall chart traced their numbers
in money's green line. It didn't
record the pain when someone
ran the needle through her finger.

I came at noon—between classes
at the state college where I read
Marx, and day-dreamed revolution—
to eat lunch with my grandmother.

Exactly at noon, there was a moment
of quiet between the machines
shutting down and the women rising
in common with their bag lunches.

They gathered at long metal tables.
High above them, a narrow strip
of eave windows gave the only sign
of weather and, sun or gloom,

let down a long flume of light
in which the women's bodies
slowly relaxed, their lunches spread
before them, and the patter of talk

began in all those different tongues—
Haitian Creole, Canadian French,
Mexican and Puerto Rican Spanish,
Polish, Romanian, English,

Jamaican English—that spoke as one
the gospel of sacrifice and hard work.
They shared frayed photographs,
smoked, spread the good news

of children and grandchildren,
this one smart as a whip, this one
taking dance lessons, this one a sight
to see hitting a baseball. There were

some they worried about collectively,
and one who actually gave up booze
and became the man of their prayers.
Many more, of course, would not

be saved no matter how hard
they worked. No end to the curses
and slammed doors, the hands
and faces bloodied by impotence

and rage. I often left the mill
wondering if their hard ritual
of work-eat-sleep-work ever changed
the state of daily lousiness at all.

The women believed, or had to
believe. Over thirty years ago,
and still I see them returning to
their machines, the unforgiving

clock running once again,
the women bending to their work,
losing themselves freely in that noisy
oblivion because each of them

cradles a secret happiness—that someone,
working at his own sweet time,
might tell the story many years later
of how he had come to be saved.

Ears of the Heart

When we are dying the last faculty usually to shut down is hearing.

St. Benedict said, *Listen with the ears of your heart.*

And so I try to remember what was once heard
in the practice of the heart's listening:
the surprise of a robin's common song

when I was ready to hear it. And wind saying itself
in the tulip leaves outside my childhood window.

So many times I've needed to learn again
what I am always forgetting—
that each thing has its own pitch and vibration and rings
with the exactness of a bell.

Like the sounds rain makes so differently
filling a tin cup or waterfalling leaf by leaf through
the understories of a forest.

And there's my mother's voice calling
me home for supper and, later, saying goodbye.

When I am dying to the world will the ears of my heart hear—

in a hospital room's trickle of sad laughter,
in the sitcom leaking down
from the television, in the doctor's voice calling my name
when no one is sure I am still listening—

the voice of my beloved moving like light
at the beginning of each day,

speaking in words I have heard but never clearly enough to write down, saying everything I could never say?

The Weeper

The name his followers gave Ignatius, who wept
while saying mass, or while listening to the coos
of a common dove. Ignatius never knew
when his throat would tighten, a wave of sobs
breaking him open as he stood watching clouds
move in the wide gaze of the sky, or passed a boy
climbing a pine, lost in the play of his body.
Yet it wasn't the reverie of blue sky and clouds,
nor even the boy's self-forgetful happiness
that brought on those tears beyond his control.
These days, when passion is cooled by irony,
when we try to live as if each day were
predictable and self determined, when God
and the soul are off-limits, how can we understand
such abandonment in a man who wept
almost daily—not because of the time he'd wasted
or would waste, not because of his weak stomach
or his leg's old war injury, or because he'd given up
the feel of trembling flesh along the inner curve
of a woman's thigh or the full, idle hours
spent in his father's castle. Not even because of
the wearied and hopeless poor whom he met
on every road and went among in cities.
He wept, they say, because he'd suddenly feel
entirely empty, and utterly grateful, all the doors
of his heart, which was and was not his
at these moments, and which we know
only as metaphor, swung wide open, able now
to receive and find room for all the world's
orphaned outpourings and astonishments.

from *Walking with Ruskin* (2011)

Dangling

When I believe I have no needs I cannot fulfill,
when my lies sound like truth,

and when I've added yet another self
to my fabrications, I contemplate the life of a monk

on Mt. Athos. It's said that he ties one end
of a rope to a cypress, then loops the other

around his chest and walks off the cliff where he lives.
Lord, you are my stronghold, he prays, dangling

a few hundred feet above the darker water
where the bottom drops off.

I suppose it's a way of restoring the grace
of insignificance, hanging like that

between the sky and the sea. I like to think
my thinking is a form of spiritual exercise,

but I never reach that moment
of unburdening when the monk feels at ease

(or so I wish), free now that he's tethered
again to God, when he needs nothing

that is not provided by the sea floating up on air,
its scent alone like the taste of the richest oysters.

No, for me, each day's fresh start points only
to the tree, the rope, the cliff-edge and sea.

And the going over, again and again.

Thirty-Second Concert

> Orcas Island, Washington

Just now,
overlapping,

the sound of water
against rock, against rock,

and, diminuendo,
with less *plock*, against driftwood,

and lower still, the ostinato
of a distant, invisible plane

playing in counterpoint
to a white-crowned sparrow's clear
first two alto notes

and the zigzag cacophony
of a kingisher's rattle—

here and gone—
passing into three caws
of a crow

as if every sound
connected to another,

or as if one sound
were making itself completely new
again and again,

even this deerfly's buzzing vibrato
one of the voices

that slide into or under
or over another,

and take place
all at once and at every moment,
though I hear it all

for no more
than thirty seconds
before the self's deafness returns.

Czeslaw Milosz's Glasses

I.

Shortly after his death, they came to me
in a blue velvet Sailor fountain pen case,

a gift from a poet-friend who found Milosz
had left his glasses behind at a poetry festival.

By the time she reached him, he had
already bought a new pair. He's wearing

them in a photograph on the back cover
of *Second Space*; he's writing a poem,

or pretending to be for the photograph.
I like to think he's listening to the *daimonion*

he sometimes heard, writing down what it said—
faithfully. Yet he scoured every poem

for the disguises he knew were his, and unavoidable,
no matter how carefully he tried to listen.

II.

His glasses fit my wide head. I like to
put them on, but when I look through them,

the spruce tree outside my window is no longer
a spruce tree, hardly a tree at all; his glasses

make my head hurt. Which is meet and right,
as the Prayer Book says, no one knowing

better than him how the eyes are a temptation.
So much evil in believing that others see

the world just as we do. He knew words
could never navigate the roundness of things,

and yet knew, too, his work was to catch
the complexity of all in one unwritable sentence

he tried to write again and again.
Such a long journey to describe things

as they are. Sunlit depths of rivers. A wood
table set with plates for dinner. The roundness

of pears. The shape of a woman's breasts under
a summer dress. And also: a Nazi putting out

a cigarette on a Jewish child's arm. A pregnant
woman lying in a Warsaw street, being kicked,

begging for the blows to end. Families taken away,
wherever they were herded to, a nowhere.

III.

I met him once. He read his poems, and after
we had dinner with some others. I never said

how much I admired him, the poems.
We talked about the Psalms, their thirst for justice,

and he said man's instinctual sense of
what ought to be was precisely (and *perversely*,

he added) what lay behind the appeal
of propaganda in the modern era, lies

always more alluring and comforting
than reality. He drank too much and, rising

from the table with his cane, stumbled
and fell—something I tell only because

I feel he, who knew his faults better than anyone,
would have wanted me to. As he approached

his 90th year, he wrote that his former lives
were like *ships departing*, that the countries, cities

and gardens he'd known all this time were "ready now
to be described better than they were before"—

as if he'd just received a new prescription,
and could see, at least for the time being,

more clearly through his newest glasses.
I keep his old glasses in my desk drawer,

and take them out at times when I begin
a poem. Not for inspiration, but for correction.

Reading George Herbert

All he ever wanted was to disappear.
But he kept coming upon himself
as if he were a character in a story
who, despite his best efforts to understand,
remained inscrutable. He tried
to keep straight the difference between
who the author said he was and who he
thought he was. He told himself again
and again that God was closer to him
than he was to himself. Still, he couldn't

close the distance. He was always getting
lost in his own plot, going off in all
the wrong directions. His own words
never helped, being always full of
a wild hunger, self-propulsive.
Prayer helped. But even when he heard
a melody not his own, when he'd try
to sing it, what came out of him
was off-key and horribly out of tune.

Each day he went to war against himself,
but he could never disarm himself.
Yet, waking, he'd often relish the new day,
tasting the sweetness of the world
he accepted as an undeserved gift.
And, in its clear and shimmering air,
he'd sometimes see a road that ran straight
to the open door of paradise,
though the moment he started walking,

the day would be diminished by the weight
of clouds that gradually lugged themselves
all the way to the horizon. How could he

not help but think, *sure, of course,
just as I expected, just what I deserved?*
Once, having traveled farther
from himself than he'd ever been,
he believed he heard God saying, *Yes, this way
come ahead, enter*, but he was only human,
and thought the voice must be his own.

Erasure

It's what I need to practice,
the lines of my life too neatly drawn
around the comfort of being here.

It's why I'm out here again,
in the middle of the field just as
the day pauses between what is

and what was, darkness rising
between the hemlocks and spruces
that have brought their shadows

together. I'm waiting for the moment
when the oaks and ashes
slip from the names we've given them,

the thrushes have had their say
and the dark adds the slightest chill
to the air, a breeze announcing itself

in the wind-chimes. It's then
that the invisible hearse of darkness
waits for me to get in. It's then

that I too often call out, *here
I am,* to someone who has just begun
to wonder where I have gone.

Shame

Four last night. They trickled into the church
before the cold solidified. My wife and I signed them in,
made them empty pockets, checked for drugs and weapons,
went over the copious medications they carried,
then let them graze on free coffee, oranges, bread,
crackers, peanut butter, even a large bag
of Kentucky Fried wings a parishioner
brought by—gifts and leftovers of our middle class.

Once a month or so in the winter, my wife and I
volunteer to open the doors and sleep on the floor
with whoever needs to come in out of the cold,
mostly castaways of the state that cuts costs
by closing down the mental hospitals. Again,
the shock of fitting their lives into ours:
how normal everyone appeared at first, and then,
inexorably, their oddnesses leaked out.

Karen—articulate, well educated—talked about
Exodus, then waved her hand suddenly to reveal five
angels that help her communicate with her children,
taken away years back: *trouble with the Feds* over her politics.
Off in the corner, Ed, who had a pocketful of meds, said
he'd married a deaf and dumb woman who played around.
When he hit her, hard, she moved to Florida.
Ed never sleeps, afraid he'll dream of her, whom he *loves*

more than life. Jim—alcoholic, depressed, unstable—
is trying to get to Florida (their crazy bond) where his father
is dying, but he doesn't know what town. And Deanna?
She came just to help out, she said, though it's clear
this group is her only family. And then what needed to be told

was told, and what could not be told moved back into
the confusion of their minds. As if they'd just remembered
no one would tell them, "It will be all right, all right,"

everyone went utterly quiet, retreating to what they do
by rote—gather blankets, wash, pee, divide themselves
into the rooms for women and men. So we slept,
heat at the center, the oil burner droning out the dream talk,
the groaning and shifting of weight. Near dawn, I saw Ed
sitting up, then leaning back on his arms as if he were caught
in a contradiction he couldn't resolve, waiting for
the morning, and wishing it would never come.

It came, the sun a disc of white in the steel-colored sky.
My wife and I locked the church, and warmed up our car.
Our group of night visitors bunched against the wall.
They could have been the brunt of God's joke
about the last who shall be first. No biblical edge
of the field left to glean, for them it's store-front
encampments, and the shuffling in and out of the cold
according to the good will and shame of the owners.

Sparrows

> A certain traveler who knew many continents
> was asked what he found most remarkable
> of all. He replied: the ubiquity of sparrows.
> —Adam Zagajewski, Another Beauty

Sparrow: our generic for any of the small brown birds
we find everywhere. A farm field in early April,
nothing yet green. Or a sidewalk downtown

edged with February's dirty snow, a scrap
of paper with someone's name on it
skittering in a gust of building-tunneled wind.

Sparrows: fussing about in the dirt, washing
themselves in a gutter's runoff, hanging on
the dry seed head of a winter weed.

Barn, strip mall, field, swamp, college ivy,
Walmart sign: all places to prove their gift for
survival. Like the poor, they are their own keepers.

Once in Palestine there were so many, two
could be had for the price of one farthing,
but Jesus said his father knew each of them,

just as the hairs on our head are numbered.
Those must have been house sparrows; they were
fruitful and multiplied because they fed on

the droppings of horses and cattle. Sparrows.
I never learned them well enough. They slipped
in and out of my focus, the color of dust

and dirt, common-featured. *Field sparrow,*
fox sparrow, song sparrow, swamp sparrow.
It took so much attention to give a name

to them, the way, too often, I see the poor
only as that, their faces hidden as they lie
like sacks on grates of vented heat. Ubiquitous.

common-featured. How can they be seen
when they are always in sight? When Jesus
laid his hands on the faces of the poor,

I'd like to believe he saw them as they wanted
to be seen: each a child who belonged
to somebody, who once had a given name.

Four Prayers

I. *March Prayer*

What do I do to keep the image of her
bent over her dead son as alive as this bluebird—
elegant and simple, and perfectly made for delight—
releasing its blue to the sky? How do I speak
of a mother bent over her son's body
as if he could still recognize it was her there
alongside him, ready to go wherever he was going . . .
and also of this morning that arrived fresh and new,
old piles of snow being eaten by a March sun,
water running everywhere, the *hey sweetie* of chickadees
leafing the leafless trees. O Lord, this is
what I know: grief is endless, delight unavoidable.
Teach me to live in this contradiction, help me
to keep seeing her desiccated mouth, the sorrow
in her throat she could not swallow, her eyes
that still, months later, cannot see
this bluebird which I cannot enjoy any less.

II. *June Prayer*

Pray for me, she said, and Lord I try.
I have no eye for eternity. I know
only this world, where May's light lengthens
into June's long days, and someone I love
keeps discovering that grief is a season
that leads nowhere. Lord, take pity
on this prayer which is meant to be plain,
to ask no more than what has always been
asked—that she be helped to bear the weight
she cannot bear alone. But I cannot refrain
from asking something more: Why,

if she can still perfectly recall the horror
she most wants to forget, why, as the months
pass, is she already losing the feel of her son's
touch and the exact timbre of his voice
when he joked with her? Lord, the sun is
stronger each day and the trees have filled
with birds again, but all she sees
are the boys she must forgive each day
for living, for bouncing a basketball or
carrying their mitts and bats. And she does.
She does. Can you not, then, help her lift
her head and say again—*Blessed is the day*—
words, perhaps, that might release her
from her season of captivity in the dark
belly of memory where she waits for you.

III. *October Prayer*

It rains, it rains, and the leaves, more brown
than gold, come off like a child's soaked
clothes. One season collapses
into another. For ten months, Lord,
I have gone down to the place where the dead
are shut away. I have wanted to speak
with the authority of *It came to pass,*
or *verily I say to you* to one I dearly love,
but I have no powers to restore the blood
that drained from the veins of her child.
Only, *this must be endured,* as if endurance
could lighten the weight of her grief.
She keeps measuring her grief against
the grief of others—one thirteen-year-old
against the thirty million children dead
each year, one son against the thousands
lost to starvation, to war, just one against
the tens of thousands lost in an earthquake.
Each day, she counts the losses; today,

a father's three young children and his wife
to a mudslide that buried their home.
Why is it, she wants to know, that one
lost son can so empty the entire world?
Why, she asks, can't she *move forward,*
find the strength, rise to the occasion,
get through it? Lord, she knows too well
she is not the center of anything,
and yet she remains, waiting still
at the place where her son left her, waiting
for the Spirit said to ease us. I have
waited for a prayer, for some words to help
her believe what can never be changed can be
endured and made easier in its suffering
as I walked in circles in these wet woods,
the leaves down, here and there another
fresh stump where a tree has fallen over
staring upwards, the lines of trees against
one another like a child's scribblings
that do not mean a thing.

IV. *December Prayer*

For seven days the sword is drawn,
for thirty days it wavers; and after
twelve months, it returns to its scabbard—
the wisdom of the Talmud, a recognition
of death's hold on the living
left behind. Lord, her year is done
and, if nothing else, your silence
has taught her daily that her son
must be given up sense by sense,
thought by thought, action by action.
Just a year and a day ago
he would have made her laugh
or argued with her or talked back.
Now December is dying once again

into the roosting dark: cold air, cold
flame, the sky burning itself clean.
Lord, I ask this much for her,
who knows too well she will go on
missing him until she dies: let rooms
made small by the violence of grief
be amplified by the wan light
the sun hoists over the inch
of new winter snow. Let there be
laughter again at the kitchen table,
let the spoons and forks make a racket
on the plates, and the youngest's
spilled glasses of milk be seen
as cups running over. Let her eyes,
blinded for so long by grief, see again
what is just outside her window:
a red and white clownish woodpecker,
two nuthatches spiraling head first
down a tree, the neighbor in her
nightgown who holds out her hands
with five different kinds of seed,
a suburban St. Francis of the birds,
and another, like Moses, waving
and honking in clouds of white exhaust
as he backs from his driveway and leads
a string of cars toward the station.
Lord, give her this day. For one year
she has waited out the empty rehearsals
of hope. And she will go on living with
the pain of what will never make sense.
But Lord, death's year is up. Let the sun
pass over her face as she sits by the window.
When the early dark arrives, let her watch
the sky orchestrate the last orange glints
the day becomes. Let that be an end of it . . .

Why I Live Here

Because the view is always partial,
small-paned, the sky parceled out by trees.

Because I like the grey and brown birds
and how they flit in and out of my vision

in the grey and brown woods,
endless versions of what can and cannot be seen.

And because I like the mystery of an old truck
that suddenly appears in the middle

of these roadless, second-growth woods,
a maple sapling growing from the windshield,

its backseat a storehouse for nuts,
a chickadee bathing on its caved-in roof.

Or how my eyes can map winter's bare-limbed roll
of hills, each lost, then found again as I walk.

Because I can sit in the woods and watch
a white-tailed deer move from one leg

to another, never once putting a foot
completely down, always ready to disappear.

Sitting there, I've noticed the brotherhood
of mosses on bark and stones,

and the intricate, beetled life of dead trees.
Still, there's always something I never quite see—

a vole (?) moving under leaves, or a grouse (I think)
that's only tail feathers disappearing into a thicket

of spirea. Where I live is good practice
at reading from the Book of Concealments.

Because the ancient stories have already said
how we can travel to the gods and back,

or emerge from the labyrinthine underworld
and still not know enough, I'm preparing

for the last page when the story some expect
to be revealed in full still surpasses understanding.

My Neighbor's Mailbox

The first time some teens, buzzed on beer
or coke, caved in her mailbox with a bat,
a new one appeared the very next day,

but with two small hand-painted geese
on the routine black metal where the flag
is raised. When that one was crushed,

her next gave both sides to a scene
of woods and field and a small brook
that joined each other at the door.

After yet a third time the mailbox
and even the post was taken out, she built
a little red barn out of wood

with a door that opened to receive
the mail. Below the mailbox, she placed
a flower pot, of deep blue porcelain,

filled with salmon-colored lilies . . .
Often I see her pulling weeds, watering
the open-throated lilies, tending to

the spot of ground around the mailbox
as if Martin Buber were right, and God allots
to each of us our own little area to redeem.

Of course her actions may only prove again
how thin the line between divinity and madness.
Or that she may be merely holding on

to some principle learned in Sunday school,
those kids no more to her than a test

of neighborly love. But maybe

she sees those boys, whoever they are,
with girlfriends and high school classes,
all of them rushing into what lies ahead

without a sense yet of who they might be;
and maybe she can imagine them
arriving one night only to pull back their bat

and just laugh, the barn door open,
a letter lying like a beast in its stall, the night air
disarming, charged with the scent of lilies.

Last Things

I am always thinking about death—
my own mostly, but this morning

Augustine's, he who asked to be left alone
at the end, his only company

the six large-lettered penitential psalms
he tacked to his cell walls, a map

even a saint needs, I guess, on the journey
toward death the self keeps trying

to prepare itself for. So often I have prayed,
Teach me the way I should go, and *O Lord,*

heal me, for my bones are shaking with terror,
as if, in the repetition of those words,

each larval stage of my life might be let go.
But just as often I have been distracted

by dust on the windowsill dimpling with rain
or the yellow shine of afternoon sun

on the grass, by the rush and babble
of voices talking all at once in the next room,

or even a dog's barking—as Augustine
may have been, looking up now and again

from his prayer, arrested by an ordinary cloud
passing across the face of the sun

and the new shadows pooling on the floor,
the next thing still happening, still arriving

and being replaced, still restless, all of it
part of a world so hard to finish loving.

Luna Moths

The first time I woke up crying
from a puddle of sleep, I found it

fluttering against a wall
like a dying leaf of spring green light.

The second, I found lying lightly
on the ground, newly dead.

I brought it inside, and placed it
on a blank piece of paper

for my study. Palest green wings.
A thin red border, like a child's outline,

on the edges of its forewings
and hindwings. A yellow inner border

on its long, tailed hindwings.
Four white eyespots, ringed in yellow

and maroon. On that white
sheet of paper, it appeared to be

some beautiful, lost metaphor
of an indecipherable language.

   ***

I'd read the facts—the one-week life span,
the way, because they do not eat,

the adults have no need of a mouth—by the time
I found the third, late at night

high on the wall of my kitchen.
I'd had too much to drink. I spoke to it

as if it were my own Buddhist teacher
here to teach me non-attachment,

the illusions of hunger, sex, rampant need.
I sat with it until the sun rose, toasting

its quick beauty, then the restfulness I found
in its body, and then those bright-eyed,

translucent green wings that seemed
to breathe more and more slowly before going

motionless. When I lifted it in my hand
I knew just how little the space was

between myself and nothingness.

Gift

> How long can one man's lifetime last?
> —Wang Wei

Long enough, he said to our tears,
to know *all of it is a gift*. We wanted
to hold him back from the dying

he was busy doing, nine months of working
his way through the Book of Subtractions:
first the relished taste of food and wine,

and then Yeats, the *Four Quartets*,
and the Psalms he could no longer read
alone. In the end, even the music

his children loaded on an I-Pod—
Mozart and Brahms to counter the morphine
that countered the bladed pains

that ran through his back—
became too difficult to listen to.
And yet he called each painful day a gift,

and held fiercely to each moment,
whatever it brought: swallows freelancing
in the wind, the odor of lilac

after a night's rain, the way sunlight settled
over the rug like a large dog—
nothing he earned, but accepted,

as he accepted the near identical looks
his children and his wife exchanged

when they saw how, daily, his cancer grew

towards the dread of his utter absence.
To all of it he said *yes*.
Yes to the pollen greening the roofs

of parked cars as his body withered,
and to the cold of the window glass
he leaned his cheek against,

and *yes,* to the nearly unendurable love
he felt for his wife and children
whose longing for him he could not

lessen, and to everything that remained
unsayable between them. And *yes,*
finally, to whatever came next, after

this life he had been given, this death.

In Between

They had reasons to believe in God.
Miracles helped. And their after-effects
must have lingered for a time, but then,
the disciples needed to start walking again,
one town to another, nothing in between
but the hot, dusty road and a desert
of sand and rock where not one thing
required a moment's appreciation.
Just one sandaled foot in front of another
and way too much time to consider
the whole bed-through-the-roof episode
or the uncrossable valley between sleeping
and death. *What did we really see?*
the disciples must have asked themselves
as they walked with their Teacher,
who always seemed near and far at once.

And what were they to make of that question
he would not stop asking, and asked,
they suspected, as if he were mocking them—
Who do you say I am, who do you say I am?
They probably wished they had more time
to think about how to answer and yet
they knew, too, that time was exactly
what they had. They must have wondered,
Is he asking, who he is or who we say he is?
And, *What does it matter who we say he is?*
Every day brought different questions—
Do we need to know who we are, to answer?
Is who we are, the same as who we are
in relation to him? And different answers.

Some days their Teacher seemed a story
that was living and some days a story
they were not sure how they would ever tell.
It could not have been easy to believe
they would be saved by someone
who told them he was headed straight
for a cross. And then it happened.
And they felt like witnesses to an event
they had never wanted, and one
that had arrived without their being
ready for it. They must have known
afterward that theirs would be
a ridiculous and mulish faith
taking place in between the arousals
of good bread and wine, and a God
who was felt most now that he was gone.

www.ingramcontent.com/pod-product-compliance
Lightning Source LLC
Chambersburg PA
CBHW020848160426
43192CB00007B/832